Key Geography for GCSE

David Waugh

Former Head of Geography
Trinity School
Carlisle

Book 2

Stanley Thornes (Publishers)

First published in 1994 by:
Stanley Thornes (Publishers) Ltd
Ellenborough House
Wellington Street
CHELTENHAM GL50 1YW
England

96 97 98 99 00 / 10 9 8 7 6 5

A catalogue record for this book is available from the British Library.
ISBN 0 7487 1671 8

Printed in Hong Kong by Dah Hua Printing Co.,Ltd.

Cover photograph: Aerial view of the confluence of
the Green and Colorado rivers, Utah
Title page photograph: Rio de Janeiro – Sugarloaf
shrouded in cloud, city and harbour

Acknowledgements

The author and publishers are grateful to the following for permission to
reproduce photographs and other copyright material in this book.

Adams Picture Library (pp. 77, C; 116, C; 120, B): Andes Press Agency (p. 43,
C): Bridgeman Art Library (p. 59, D): Cephas (pp. 4, A; 70, B; 73, F; 74, B;
79, E): Commonwealth Institute, Scotland (p. 47, F): Eye Ubiquitous (p. 63,
C): Frank Lane Picture Agency (pp. 5, F; 14, B; 35, C; 50, C; 51, F): General
Motors Corporation (p. 85, D): Catherine Hurst (p. 65, B (top)): Hutchison
Picture Library (pp. 5, E; 92, A; 93, D; 94, B; 94, C; 95, D; 95, E; 102, D):
Intermediate Technology (pp. 46, C; 115, E): Michael Busselle's Photo Library
(p. 72, E): NHPA (pp. 46, B; 50, D): Nature Photographers (pp. 14, C; 37, C;
46, B; 50, A): David Noble (p. 74, A): Oxfam (pp. 45 (right); 47, D): Panos
(pp. 31, E; 41, D; 41, E): David Paterson (p. 44, B): Rex Features (pp. 91, C;
91, E): Robert Harding Picture Library (pp. 4, B; 40, A; 56, B; 64, A (bottom);
70, C; 77, D; 87, E; 116, B): Science Photo Library (pp. 77, E, 88, A):
Spectrum Colour Library (pp. 37, B; 56, A; 57, C; 58, C; 59, E; 64, A (bottom);
65, B; 71, E; 72, A; 72, C; 72, D; 79, C; 79, D): Still Pictures (pp. 31, D; 33, B;
33, C; 35, B; 38, C; 45 (left); 46, A; 49, D; 49, E; 63, D; 71, F; 101, D; 102,
C; 103, F; 104, A; 104, B; 111, D (left and right); 115, D): Sue Cunningham
Photographic (p. 105, D): Marion and Tony Morrison South American Pictures
(pp. 103, E; 105, C): Tony Stone Worldwide (pp. cover; title page; 101, D):
University of Dundee (pp. 14, A; 16, A; 17, C): Volkswagen, Brazil (p. 106,
B): David Waugh (pp. 54, C and D; 55, E; 58, B): WWF-Worldwide Fund for
Nature (formerly World Wildlife Fund) (p. 51, E): Zefa (pp. 85, C; 89, D).
The author would like to thank Duncan Waugh for his contribution to pages
124-127.
Every effort has been made to contact copyright holders and we apologise if
any have been overlooked.

▶ Contents ◀

▶ How is weather measured and recorded? ◀

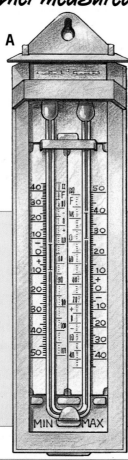

A

Weather is the day to day condition of the atmosphere. It includes temperature, precipitation, pressure, wind speed and wind direction. These climatic elements are measured, usually once a day, by reading a group of scientific instruments - the maximum and minimum thermometer (diagram **A**), rain gauge (diagram **B**), barograph (diagram **C**), anemometer (diagram **E**) and wind vane (diagram **F**).

Temperature is measured, in °C (degrees celsius), by a **maximum and minimum** (six's) thermometer. During the day the alcohol heats up and expands, pushing the mercury higher on the maximum scale. At night the alcohol cools down and contracts so the mercury reads lower on the minimum scale. In each case the position of the extreme temperature is recorded by a pin. The pins have to be drawn back (reset) to the mercury each day using a magnet. On the thermometer shown, the maximum was 28°C and the minimum 8°C.

B

Rainfall is measured using a **rain gauge**. This is a metal cylinder which contains a collecting bottle and a funnel. It is partly sunk into the ground for stability in the wind, away from trees and buildings which would shelter it and the rim is 30mm above ground level to avoid splashing. The rainwater is transferred to a measuring glass and recorded in millimetres (mm).

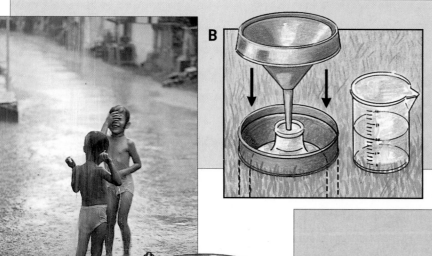

Pressure is recorded on a **barograph**. The metal cylinder contains a vacuum. Attached to it is a lever and a pen. The pen records onto graph paper attached to a rotating drum. As air pressure increases (or decreases), the cylinder is pressed downwards (or rises) raising (or lowering) the lever and pen. Air pressure is recorded in millibars (mb).

C

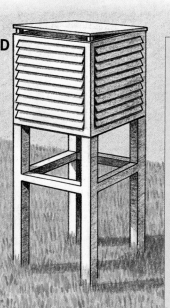

D

The **Stevenson screen** stores several of these meteorological instruments. It is painted white to reflect sunlight, and has slatted (louvred) sides to allow the free circulation of the air and to keep out direct sunlight. It is located away from buildings which could give too much protection. It is placed on grass.

Wind speed is measured by an **anemometer**. This may be attached to a building or used manually. It consists of a series of cups which rotate faster and faster as the force of the wind increases. Wind speed can be recorded either in knots or on a force scale of 0 to 12.

E

Wind direction is measured by a **wind vane**. The arrow points to the direction from which the wind blows. In the example the wind is from the north-east.

F

If weather measurements are recorded over a period of time, usually 30 years, we get the average conditions for a place. These average conditions give the expected **climate**. In Britain, for example, we expect to get cool summers, mild winters and rain throughout the year. What we actually get is often different to what we expect!

Activities

1 What is the difference between weather and climate?

2 a) Name the scientific instrument used to measure each of the following:
   - temperature,
   - precipitation,
   - air pressure,
   - wind speed,
   - wind direction.
   b) Describe the method of recording each one.

3 a) Using the scientific instruments named in Activity 2, measure and record accurately the weather for a period of one week.
   b) Record your results by either drawing graphs or producing them on a computer.

Summary

By measuring and recording daily weather conditions over a lengthy period of time it is possible to give a generalised description of the long term climate of a place.

▶ *What are the seasonal differences in climate in Britain?* ◀

Britain has a variable climate. This means that the weather changes from day to day which makes it difficult to forecast accurately. Britain's average climate, as described on page 5, is cool summers, mild winters and rain spread evenly throughout the year. However, it should be pointed out that not **every**

- year will have a cool summer, a mild winter, or an even distribution of rainfall;
- place will be cool, or mild, or wet at the same time.

In other words, the British Isles have annual, seasonal and regional variations in climate.

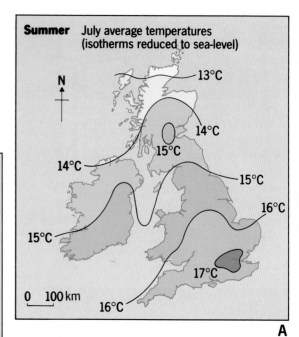

A

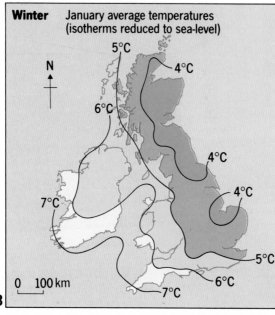

B

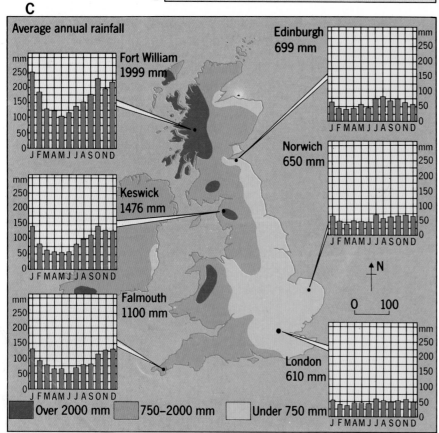

C

The seasonal distribution of temperature

Maps **A** and **B** show **isotherms** for July (summer) and January (winter). An isotherm is a line drawn on a map joining all places which have the same temperature. Isotherms usually ignore the actual height of places and are reduced to sea-level. This makes it easier to both recognise patterns on a map and to make comparisons between places.

Summer The isotherms on map **A** show that temperatures:

- are highest in the south-east of England;
- decrease from south to north;
- are higher over land than over the sea.

Winter The isotherms on map **B** show that temperatures:

- are highest in the south-west of England;
- decrease from west to east;
- are higher over the sea than over land.

The reasons for the seasonal and regional differences in temperature in the British Isles are explained on pages 8 and 9.

The annual and seasonal distribution of rainfall

Map **C** shows the expected amounts of rainfall over the British Isles in an average year. It is accompanied by six graphs. Three are for places in the west of Britain and three are for places in the east. The map and graphs show that annual rainfall totals:

- are highest in the north-west of Scotland;
- decrease rapidly from the north-west of Scotland to the south-east of England.

The graphs also show a contrast in the seasonal distribution of rainfall. Whereas places in the west receive most rain during winter (October to February), places in the east tend to get most rain in summer (July). The reasons for the annual and seasonal differences in rainfall in the British Isles are explained on pages 10 and 11.

Map **D** shows the British Isles divided into four quarters. The quarters were obtained by following two isotherms:

- the 5°C January isotherm, which divides the milder west and the colder east in winter;
- the 15°C July isotherm, which divides the warmer south from the cooler north in the summer.

The resultant map shows, in a simplified form, the seasonal and regional differences in climate in the British Isles.

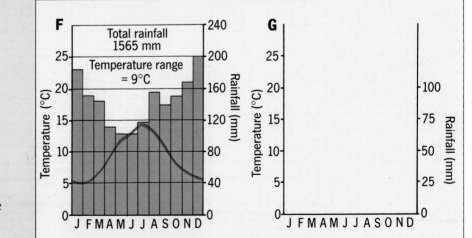

North-west Britain
Cool summers
Mild winters
Small temperature range = 9°C
Heavy rain all year

5°C

North-east Britain
Cool summers
Cold winters
Average temperature range = 11°C
Steady rain all year

N

15°C

South-west Britain
Warm summers
Mild winters
Small temperature range = 10°C
Heavy rain all year

0   100 km

South-east Britain
Very warm summers
Cold winters
Large temperature range = 14°C
Light rain all year

D

E

	Jan	Feb	Mar	Apr	May	June	July	Aug	Sep	Oct	Nov	Dec
Temperature (°C)	4	5	7	9	12	15	18	17	15	12	8	5
Rainfall (mm)	48	42	36	44	48	38	60	56	48	54	56	46

Activities

1 a) Copy and complete graph **G** by adding the information from table **E**.

2 a) Which two of the four quarters in diagram **D** do you think graph **F** and graph **G** fit?
   b) Give five reasons for your answer, referring to:
   - January temperatures,
   - July temperatures,
   - annual temperature range,
   - total rainfall,
   - season with most rainfall.

3 Copy and complete table **H** by ranking the four quarters named on diagram **D**.

F
Total rainfall 1565 mm
Temperature range = 9°C
Temperature (°C)
Rainfall (mm)
J F M A M J J A S O N D

G
Temperature (°C)
Rainfall (mm)
J F M A M J J A S O N D

H

Britain	North-west	North-east	South-west	South-east
Warmest in summer				
Mildest in winter				
Highest range in temperature				
Most rainfall				

Summary

The British Isles is said to have cool summers, mild winters and rain spread throughout the year. However, these seasonal patterns of climate vary from year to year and from region to region.

► *What factors affect temperature?* ◄

The maps on pages 6 and 7 showed significant seasonal differences in temperature between places in the British Isles. On a larger world scale, these differences in temperature are even greater. There are several reasons why, for example:

- the south of Britain is warmer than the north in summer
- the west of Britain is warmer than the east in winter
- some parts of the world of much warmer than others.

Latitude

Places which are near to the Equator are much warmer than places which are near to the poles. This is due to a combination of the curvature of the earth, the angle of the sun in the sky, and the layer of atmosphere which surrounds the earth (diagram **A**). At the Equator the sun is always at a high angle in the sky. When it is overhead it shines vertically downwards. Its heat is concentrated upon a small area which, as a result, warms up rapidly and becomes very hot. Going towards the poles, the sun's angle in the sky decreases. As the rays now have a greater area to heat, it will take the land longer to warm up and temperatures will remain much lower than those at the Equator. The atmosphere surrounding the earth contains dust, smoke and other solid particles. These particles absorb heat. As the sun's rays pass through the atmosphere at a more direct angle, and therefore more quickly, at the Equator than nearer the poles, then less heat will be lost. These are the main reasons why places in the south of Britain are warmer than places further north in summer (map **A**, page 6), and why equatorial areas are warmer throughout the year than the British Isles.

A

Atmosphere

Sun's rays are parallel. Equal amounts of heat from the sun.

Less atmosphere to pass through

More atmosphere to pass through

North Pole

Britain

Greater curvature – greater area of land to heat up

Equator

Directly above earth. Small area to heat up

Greatest curvature – very large area to heat up

South Pole

Distance from the sea

Liquids are less dense than solids. Consequently the sea will be less dense than the land, and so heat from the sun can penetrate through the water to a greater depth. As the sea moves, it allows heat to be transferred downwards. In comparison only the extreme surface of the land heats up. This means that the sea will take much longer to heat up than the land in summer but, once warmed, it will retain its heat for much longer in winter. This is why places which are near to the coast are much cooler than places inland in summer, but are warmer than places inland in winter. This explains the shape of the 15°C July isotherm for Britain (map **A**, page 6), and why the west of Britain is warmer than the east in winter (map **B**, page 6). It also explains why Britain has a small annual range in temperature (map **B**).

B

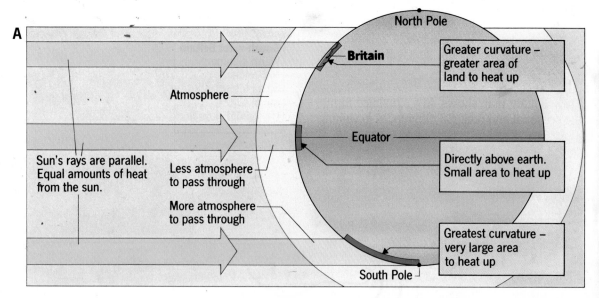

Valencia Island
Orenburg 9 • 50°N
50°N
1 •
2 •
Fishguard
London
3 •
4 • Brussels
Berlin 5 •
Warsaw 6 •
Kiev 7 •
8 • Volgograd

	1	2	3	4	5	6	7	8	9
January (°C)	8	6	4	2	−1	−3	−6	−10	−16
July (°C)	15	16	17	17	18	19	20	21	22

Prevailing winds

The temperature of the wind depends upon the type of surface over which it passes. If the prevailing wind blows from the land, it will be warm in summer but cold in winter. If, as in Britain, the prevailing wind comes from the sea, it will lower temperatures in summer but raise them in winter (diagram **C**). This also helps to explain why places in the west of Britain have cooler summers, milder winters and a smaller annual range of temperature than places further east.

C

Season	Sea	West coast	Land	East coast	Sea	Season
Winter	Warm	Warm wind ➡	**Cold**	➡ Cold wind	Warm	Winter
Summer	Cool	Cool wind ➡	**Warm**	Warm wind ➡	Cool	Summer

Relief of the land (altitude)

Mountains have much lower temperatures than the lowlands which surround them. Temperatures decrease, on average, by 10°C for every 1000 metres of height. This is because there are fewer solid particles in the upper air to retain the heat, and so the heat is rapidly lost into space. This explains why snow lies for several months each winter in the Scottish Highlands and throughout the year on several high mountains on the Equator (e.g. Mts Kenya and Kilimanjaro in Africa, and Mts Chimborazo and Cotopaxi in South America).

Aspect

Aspect is the direction in which the land, a slope or a building faces. For example, places in Britain facing the west will be warmer in winter than places facing the east. Aspect, which often has an important effect on local climates, is an example of a **microclimate** (diagram **D**).

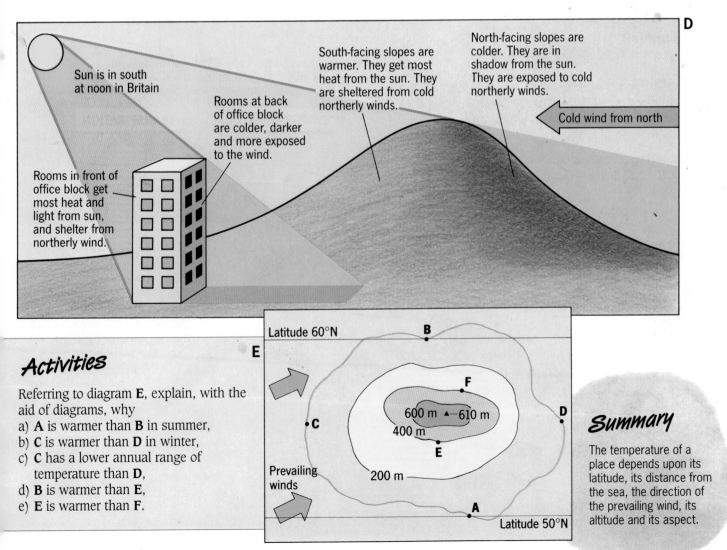

D

Sun is in south at noon in Britain

Rooms at back of office block are colder, darker and more exposed to the wind.

South-facing slopes are warmer. They get most heat from the sun. They are sheltered from cold northerly winds.

North-facing slopes are colder. They are in shadow from the sun. They are exposed to cold northerly winds.

Cold wind from north

Rooms in front of office block get most heat and light from sun, and shelter from northerly wind.

E

Latitude 60°N

Prevailing winds

600 m ▲ 610 m
400 m
200 m

Latitude 50°N

Activities

Referring to diagram **E**, explain, with the aid of diagrams, why
a) **A** is warmer than **B** in summer,
b) **C** is warmer than **D** in winter,
c) **C** has a lower annual range of temperature than **D**,
d) **B** is warmer than **E**,
e) **E** is warmer than **F**.

Summary

The temperature of a place depends upon its latitude, its distance from the sea, the direction of the prevailing wind, its altitude and its aspect.

▶ *What are the main types of rainfall?* ◀

Map **C** on page 6 described the uneven distribution of rainfall over the British Isles, but it did not attempt to give reasons for this. It did not ask why, for example:

- Britain receives rainfall throughout the year;
- the west of Britain receives more rainfall than the east;
- places in the west receive most rainfall during winter (October to January);
- places in the east often have July as their wettest month.

Diagram **A** shows the several stages in the rainmaking process. Britain receives three types of rainfall - **relief** (diagram **B**), **frontal** (diagram **C**) and **convectional** (diagram **D**). In each case warm, moist air is forced to rise and cool. Condensation causes rain to form or snow, if the temperature is below freezing point. The main difference between the three types of rainfall is what causes, or forces, the warm air to rise.

Relief rainfall

Britain receives relief rainfall throughout the year due to the

- prevailing south-westerly winds which bring warm, moist air from the Atlantic Ocean;
- presence of coastal mountains which force the air to rise and cool.

West coasts receive more rain than east coasts because the prevailing winds come from the south-west.

A

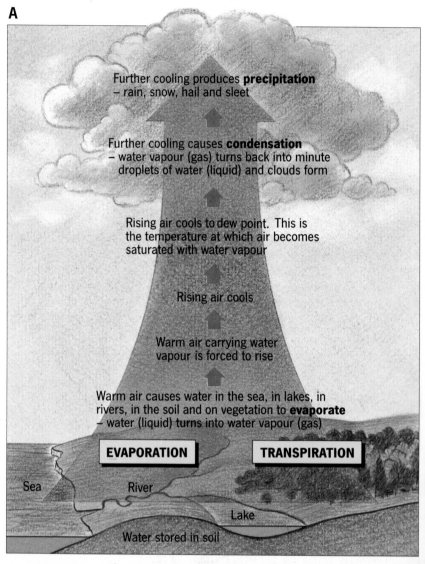

Further cooling produces **precipitation** – rain, snow, hail and sleet

Further cooling causes **condensation** – water vapour (gas) turns back into minute droplets of water (liquid) and clouds form

Rising air cools to dew point. This is the temperature at which air becomes saturated with water vapour

Rising air cools

Warm air carrying water vapour is forced to rise

Warm air causes water in the sea, in lakes, in rivers, in the soil and on vegetation to **evaporate** – water (liquid) turns into water vapour (gas)

EVAPORATION   **TRANSPIRATION**

Sea   River   Lake

Water stored in soil

B

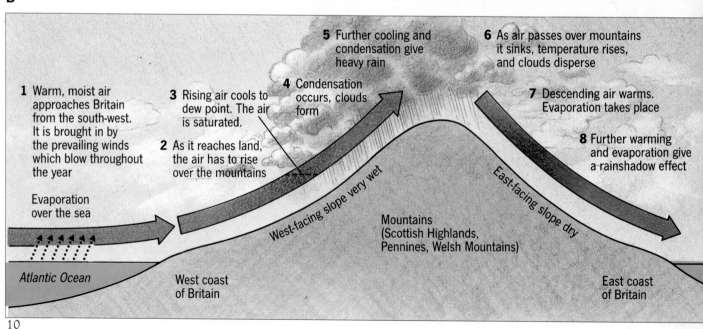

1 Warm, moist air approaches Britain from the south-west. It is brought in by the prevailing winds which blow throughout the year

Evaporation over the sea

2 As it reaches land, the air has to rise over the mountains

3 Rising air cools to dew point. The air is saturated.

4 Condensation occurs, clouds form

5 Further cooling and condensation give heavy rain

6 As air passes over mountains it sinks, temperature rises, and clouds disperse

7 Descending air warms. Evaporation takes place

8 Further warming and evaporation give a rainshadow effect

West-facing slope very wet

East-facing slope dry

Mountains (Scottish Highlands, Pennines, Welsh Mountains)

Atlantic Ocean   West coast of Britain   East coast of Britain

Frontal rainfall

Frontal rain results from the meeting of a warm mass of air and a cold mass of air. As the two air masses have different temperatures, they will have different densities and so do not mix easily. The boundary between warm and cold air is called a front. As warm air is lighter than cold air, it is forced to rise over the cold air. In Britain frontal rain occurs in depressions which form to the west of the country, over the Atlantic Ocean (page 12). In a depression warm, moist air from the tropics is forced to rise over colder, drier air from polar regions. Depressions:

- usually approach the British Isles from the south-west and so give more rain to western parts of Britain;
- are more frequent in winter which explains why western parts of Britain receive most of their rainfall during that season.

Convectional rainfall

Convectional rainfall is caused by the sun heating the ground. The heated ground will, in turn, warm the air which is in contact with it. As the air warms, it gets lighter and is forced to rise in strong upward convection currents. Water on the ground's surface will evaporate and will also rise. As the warm, moist air rises in convection currents, it cools and often gives thunderstorms. Convectional rainfall, which occurs most afternoons on the Equator (page 18), is most likely when the sun is at a high angle in the sky. Britain is usually too cool for this type of rainfall apart from places in the east and south-east which have the highest summer temperatures (map **A**, page 6). This explains why places in the east of Britain often have July as their wettest month.

C

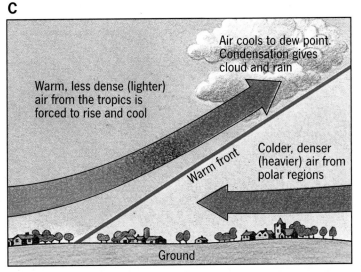

Air cools to dew point. Condensation gives cloud and rain

Warm, less dense (lighter) air from the tropics is forced to rise and cool

Warm front

Colder, denser (heavier) air from polar regions

Ground

D

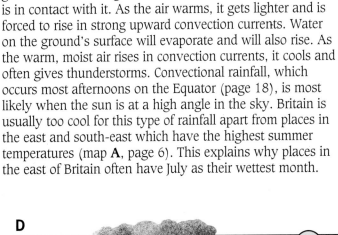
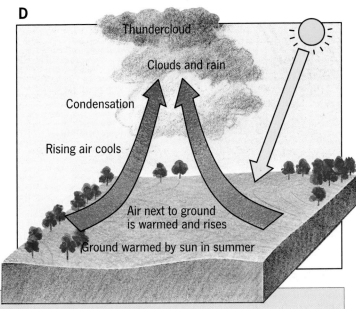

Thundercloud

Clouds and rain

Condensation

Rising air cools

Air next to ground is warmed and rises

Ground warmed by sun in summer

Activities

1 a) Put the following phrases in their correct order to answer the question, 'Why does it rain?'
rising air cools · further cooling gives condensation · warm air and water are forced to rise · warm air causes water in the sea and lakes to evaporate · further cooling causes precipitation · air is cooled to dew point

   b) Give three ways by which warm, moist air is forced to rise.

2 Along the top of table **E** are several factors which affect the distribution of rainfall in the British Isles. Copy the table and tick the appropriate boxes to show which of these factors affect the three distributions listed in the left hand column.

E

	Prevailing south-west wind	Mountains on western side of Britain	Depressions come from the Atlantic Ocean	Depressions are most frequent in winter	Convectional thunderstorms
West of Britain gets more rain than the east					
Places in the west get most of their rain in winter					
Places in the east often have July as their wettest month					

Summary

Rain is caused by warm, moist air being forced to rise and cool. The three main types of rainfall in the British Isles are relief, frontal and convectional.

11

▶ What is the weather like in a depression? ◀

Britain's weather, for much of the year, is dominated by the passing of **depressions**. Depressions are areas of low pressure which usually bring rain, cloud and wind to the British Isles.

Most depressions develop to the west of the British Isles over the Atlantic Ocean. This is where a mass of warm, moist tropical air from the south meets a mass of colder, drier polar air from the north. The two air masses, because they have different temperatures, have different densities (weight). This prevents them from mixing easily (page 11). Instead, the warmer air, which is less dense (lighter) is forced to rise over the more dense (heavier) colder air. As the warm air rises it creates an area of low pressure at ground level. The boundary between two air masses is called a front. There are two fronts in a typical depression.

1 The warm front, which passes first, is where the advancing warm air is forced to rise over the cold air.
2 The cold front, which follows, is where the advancing cold air undercuts the warm air in front of it.

In both cases the warm, moist air is forced to rise. If it cools to dew point it condenses to form cloud and to give frontal rain (page 11). Although each depression is unique, the usual weather which they bring on their eastward journey across the British Isles has an easily identifiable pattern (diagram **A**).

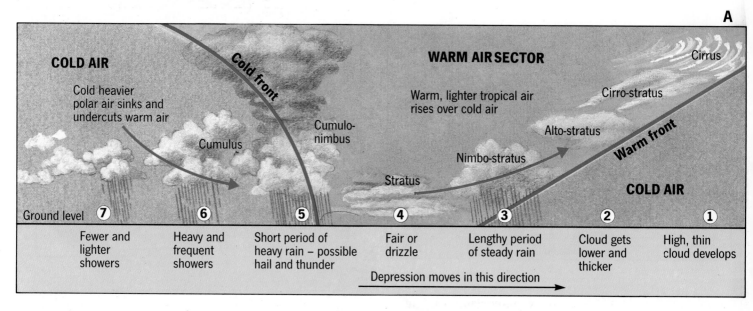

A

| ⑦ Fewer and lighter showers | ⑥ Heavy and frequent showers | ⑤ Short period of heavy rain – possible hail and thunder | ④ Fair or drizzle | ③ Lengthy period of steady rain | ② Cloud gets lower and thicker | ① High, thin cloud develops |

Depression moves in this direction

The first sign of the approaching warm front of a depression is the formation of high, thin clouds (cirrus). In time the clouds get lower and thicker (stratus). Winds slowly begin to increase in strength and blow in an anti-clockwise direction from the south-east. As warm air rises there is a rapid fall in atmospheric pressure. As the warm front passes, temperatures rise and winds become stronger blowing from a south-westerly direction. A lengthy period of steady rain falls from the low, thick clouds (nimbo-stratus).

The weather within the warm sector is less predictable. Light rain or drizzle may continue, or the clouds may break to give weak sunshine. Winds usually decrease in strength.

The most extreme conditions occur as the cold front passes. Winds often reach gale force and swing round to the north-west. Rainfall is very heavy, and can at times be accompanied by hail and even thunder (cumulo-nimbus clouds). The rain, however, is of shorter duration than that at the warm front. As the cold air replaces the warm air, temperatures fall and atmospheric pressure rises. In time the heavy rain gives way to frequent and heavy showers and winds slowly begin to decrease in strength. Temperatures remain low due to the winds which continue to come from the north-west. Eventually the showers die out and the clouds disperse to give increasingly longer sunny intervals. Usually, however, this is just a short lull before the approach of the next depression and the repetition of a similar weather sequence. An average depression can take between one and three days to pass over the British Isles.

Diagram **A** is a section, viewed from ground level, through a typical depression. Diagram **B** shows three weather maps, viewed from the air, drawn at different times during the passing of a depression. Weather maps have their own weather symbols (page 15). In diagram **B** the warm front is shown by the red line and the cold front by the blue line. The black 'circular' lines are **isobars**. Isobars are lines which join up places of equal pressure. The closer together the isobars are on a weather map, the stronger the wind will be.

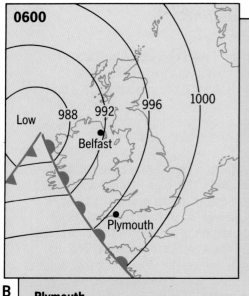

0600

Low 988 992 996 1000
Belfast
Plymouth

1200

1000 996 992 988
Low
Belfast
Plymouth

1800

N
996 992 988 Low
Belfast
Plymouth

B

Plymouth
Dry and sunny. Light clouds approaching from west. Winds gentle but increasing from the south-east.
Temperatures expected to rise.

Plymouth
Cloudy with steady rain.
Strong winds from the south-west.
Warm.

Plymouth
Stormy weather.
Gale force winds from the north-west.
Heavy rain giving way to showers.
Colder, becoming brighter later.

Activities

1 a) Make a copy of diagram **C**.
   b) Mark and label the following:
      - warm front   • area of low pressure
      - cold front   • lengthy period of steady rain
      - warm sector (warm air) • short period of heavy rain.

2 Use diagrams **A** and **B**, together with the written information on these two pages, to complete table **D** to describe the weather associated with the passing of a typical depression.

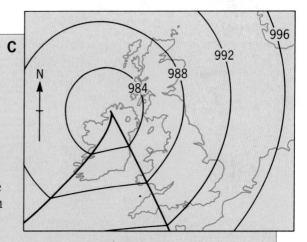

C

N
996 992 988 984

⑤ After the cold front passes	④ As cold front passes	③ During the warm sector	② As warm front passes	① As the warm front approaches	Weather conditions	
					Temperature	**D**
					Pressure	
					Cloud amount and type	
					Precipitation	
					Wind direction	
					Wind speed	

3 Use diagram **B** to:
   a) Describe the weather conditions at Belfast for 0600 hours, 1200 hours (noon) and 1800 hours.
   b) Explain why the weather at Belfast changed during this period of time.
   c) Give a short forecast for the expected weather at Belfast 0000 hours (midnight).

Summary

Britain's weather is dominated by the passing of depressions. These form when warm, moist air meets colder, drier air. They are areas of low pressure which bring cloud, rain and wind to the British Isles.

▶ *What is the weather like in an anticyclone?* ◀

A Satellite photo of an anticyclone

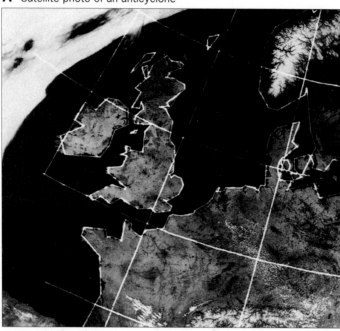

Anticyclones are areas of high pressure. They affect the British Isles far less frequently than do depressions. The weather associated with them is the opposite to that brought by depressions. Once anticyclones develop, also unlike depressions, they tend to remain stationary for several days giving very dry, bright and settled conditions.

Anticyclones form in places where the air is descending. As more and more air descends, the 'higher' will become the atmospheric pressure. Descending air is also warming air which means that it can pick up more moisture through evaporation. As condensation is unlikely in these conditions, clouds rarely form and the weather remains fine and dry (photo **A**). Wind speeds are usually very gentle and at times may die away altogether to give a period of calm. Winds blow in a clockwise direction.

There are, however, important seasonal differences in the typical weather associated with anticyclones. In summer, when the sun is higher in the sky, temperatures rise quickly and daytimes are hot and sunny (photo **B**). At night the clear sky allows the heat to escape and temperatures can fall rapidly. As it is the ground surface which loses heat, some condensation can occur to give dew and mist. The dew and mist soon disperse when the sun rises the next day. During winter, when the sun is at a low angle in the sky, daytime temperatures remain low but the weather will be dry and bright. At night, the clear skies again allow a rapid loss of heat. Condensation at ground level at this time of year leads to the formation of frost and fog (photo **C**). These may persist for all, or most of, the next day due to the sun's lack of heat.

B Weather in a summer anticyclone

Synoptic charts

Synoptic charts are maps which can show several weather conditions at one particular time, e.g. midday. The weather conditions can include temperatures, pressure, cloud cover, types of precipitation, wind speeds and wind direction. The daily weather map as shown on television or in a newspaper (map **D**) aims to give a clear, visual and simplified forecast. Synoptic maps issued by the Meteorological Office use official symbols which give weather conditions at specific weather stations (diagram **E**). Each station (diagram **F**) shows five weather conditions while a sixth, atmospheric pressure, can be obtained by interpreting the isobars.

C Weather in a winter anticyclone

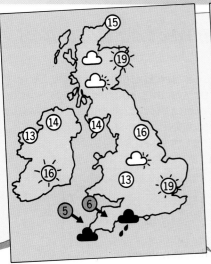

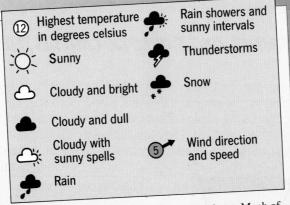

D

⑫ Highest temperature in degrees celsius	Rain showers and sunny intervals
☀ Sunny	Thunderstorms
☁ Cloudy and bright	Snow
☁ Cloudy and dull	
☁ Cloudy with sunny spells	➎ Wind direction and speed
🌧 Rain	

Britain today: Scotland will be cloudy and wet. Much of England and Wales will have sunny spells and showers, but southern England will become cloudy and wet later.

E

Official weather symbols

Present weather
- = Mist
- ≡ Fog
- , Drizzle
- ; Rain and drizzle
- • Rain
- ✻ Snow
- ▽ Rain shower
- ⚹ Snow shower
- ⊖ Hail shower
- R Thunderstorm

Wind speed (knots)
- ◎ Calm
- 1–2
- 3–7
- 8–12
- 13–17
- For each additional half-feather add 5 knots
- 48–52

Wind direction
Arrow showing direction wind is blowing from
i.e. ⟶ west

Temperature
Shown in degrees celsius
i.e. 15°

Cloud
- ○ Clear sky
- 1/8 covered
- 2/8 covered
- 3/8 covered
- 4/8 covered
- 5/8 covered
- 6/8 covered
- 7/8 covered
- ● 8/8 covered
- ⊗ Sky obscured

Fronts
- Warm
- Cold
- Occluded

F

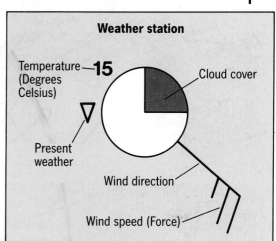

Weather station

Temperature (Degrees Celsius) — **15**
Cloud cover
Present weather
Wind direction
Wind speed (Force)

Activities

1 Photo **A** was taken during the middle of a day in June. Give an accurate and detailed weather forecast for England and Wales for the afternoon of that same day.

2 The weather conditions in a depression and an anticyclone are very different. Make an enlarged copy and complete table **G** to show the main differences.

3 a) Describe five weather conditions at the two weather stations shown in diagram **H**.
  b) Draw two weather stations and add the following weather information:
   i) Place **X**: temperature – 26 °C; present weather – mist; wind direction – NE; wind speed – force 1; cloud cover – 1/8 covered.
   ii) Place **Y**: temperature – 12 °C; present weather – rain; wind direction – SW; wind speed – force 8; cloud cover – 8/8 covered.

G

	Depression	Anticyclone	
Pressure			
Wind direction			
Wind speed			
Cloud cover			
		Summer	Winter
Precipitation			
Temperature			

H

Station **R** — 18
Station **S** — 6

Summary

Anticyclones are areas of high pressure which usually give lengthy periods of fine, dry and settled weather. Synoptic charts are used to show the weather conditions for a particular place at a given moment of time.

▶ *Interpreting cloud patterns and synoptic charts from weather satellites* ◀

Synoptic charts are often issued along with **satellite images** (photos **A** and **C**; maps **B** and **D**). Satellite images are photos taken from space and sent back to earth. They are essential when trying to produce a weather forecast or for making short term predictions about likely changes in the weather. Satellite photos, which usually have lines of latitude and longitude superimposed upon them, show images of cloud patterns (photo **A**).

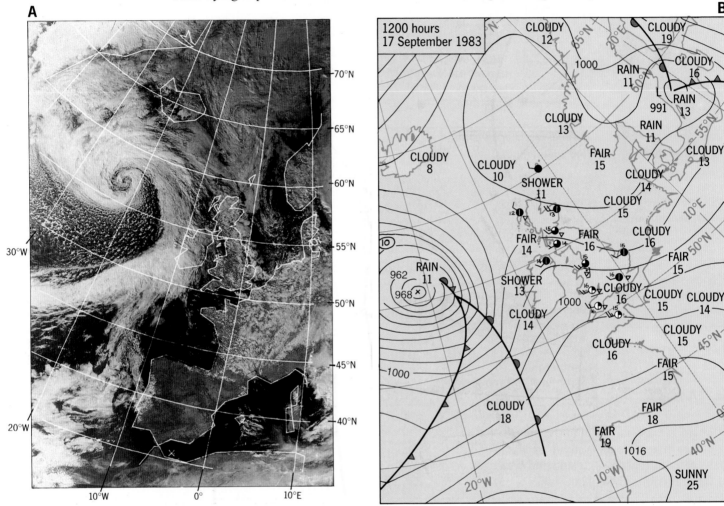

Photo **A** shows a typical depression approaching the British Isles. It was taken two and a half hours before synoptic chart **B**. The cloud pattern, in white on the photo, shows the points listed below.

- The centre of the depression is a mass of swirling cloud (latitude 57°N, longitude 22°W).
- The warm front is a thickening band of cloud which is beginning to obscure the coastline of Ireland. The warm front, marking the advance of the depression, lies to the east of the cold front.
- The cold front is a long tail of cloud extending south-westwards back into the Atlantic Ocean.

- The occluded front is a very thick band of cloud resulting from the cold front having caught up with the warm front. As there is no warm sector in an occlusion, there is no chance of any clearing skies as is possible between the fronts of some depressions.
- A band of heavy showers, shown as patches of cloud, follow behind the cold front (between latitude 50° to 55°N and longitude 15° to 30°W).

Photo **A** also shows an area of clear skies over Spain and the Western Mediterranean which indicates the existence of an anticyclone.

Photo **C** is part of a sequence of satellite images which were taken to show the passage of the depression shown in photo **A**. It was taken 24 hours after photo **A**. The full sequence of images indicated the direction and the speed at which the cloud, and therefore the depression, moved. Forecasters use information from satellite images together with data collected from weather stations on land and weather ships at sea, to draw synoptic charts (maps **B** and **D**). By relating satellite images to synoptic charts forecasters are able to describe and interpret changes in the weather.

C

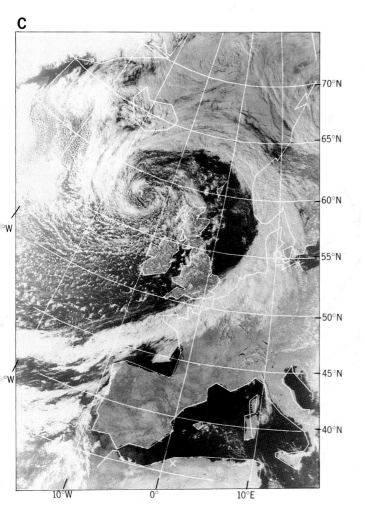

D

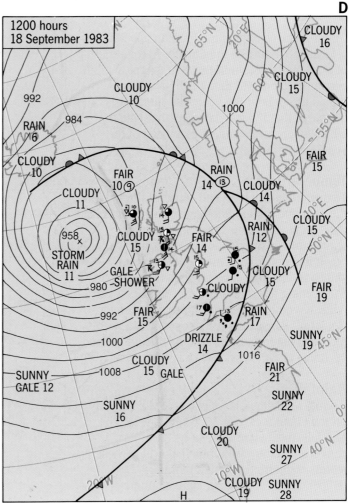

Activities

1 What is the difference between a satellite image and a synoptic chart?

2 Match up the cloud patterns shown in photo **A** and in the description on page 16 with synoptic chart **B**.

3 Describe and give reasons for the changes in
   a) cloud pattern,
   b) weather conditions
   over the British Isles between 1200 hours on 17 September, 1983 and 1200 hours on 18 September, 1983.

4 How did the weather over Spain differ from that over England and Wales during the period of the forecast?

Summary

Satellite images are photos taken from space and relayed back to earth. They show cloud patterns which, together with synoptic charts, help forecasters to describe and to predict the weather.

▶ The equatorial climate ◀

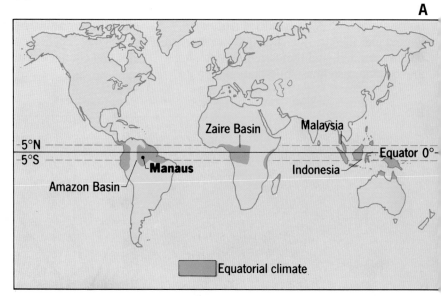

A

Equatorial climate

Places with an equatorial climate lie in a narrow zone which extends roughly 5° either side of the Equator (map **A**). The zone is not, however, continuous. It is broken by the Andes Mountains in South America and the East African Plateau in Africa.

Graph **B** is a climate graph for Manaus. Manaus is located 3° south of the Equator in the centre of the Amazon Basin in Brazil. It is typical of an equatorial climate in that it is hot, wet and humid throughout the year. The climate is unique in that it has a daily weather pattern which is repeated virtually every day of the year, and no seasons.

Temperatures

Temperatures are high and constant throughout the year and the annual range of temperature is very small (2°C). The major influence on temperature is the position of the sun. Even when it is not directly overhead, it always shines from a very high angle in the sky (page 8). Evening temperatures rarely fall below 22°C while daytime temperatures, due to afternoon cloud and rain, rarely rise above 32°C. Places on the Equator receive 12 hours of daylight and 12 hours of darkness every day of the year.

Rainfall

Annual rainfall totals for places located directly on the Equator exceed 2000 mm a year. The rain falls most afternoons in heavy convectional thunderstorms (page 11). These storms result from the high morning temperatures evaporating large amounts of water from the many rivers and swamps, and from the rainforest vegetation. Manaus, because it is 3° from the Equator, has a short, drier (but not dry) season when the overhead sun has 'moved' to a position north of the Equator. Heavy dew forms during most nights.

Although equatorial areas experience strong vertical air movements, surface winds are light and variable. There are no prevailing winds.

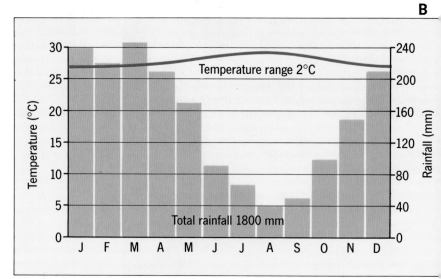

B

Temperature range 2°C

Total rainfall 1800 mm

Activities

1 a) Describe the location of those places with an equatorial climate.
  b) Name, with the help of an atlas, four countries with an equatorial climate.
  c) Give four differences between the climate graph for Manaus and a climate graph for a place in your home region.

2 Why do equatorial climates have:
  a) high temperatures throughout the year and a low annual temperature range?
  b) heavy convectional thunderstorms during most afternoons?

Summary

Equatorial climates, which are hot, wet and humid throughout the year, are usually located within 5° north or south of the Equator and where there is low relief.

▶ Hot desert climates ◀

Hot deserts are, with the exception of the Sahara which extends across Africa, located mainly on west coasts of continents between latitudes 15° and 30° north and south of the Equator (map **C**). Graphs **D** and **E** are climate graphs for two places in the Sahara. Graph **D** is Cape Juby (28°N) on the Atlantic coast in southern Morocco. Graph **E** is for Khartoum (15°N) in the Sudan. Although both places have limited rainfall, there is a considerable difference in their temperatures.

Temperatures

Temperatures are highest when the sun is directly overhead at the Tropic of Cancer, and cooler when it is in the opposite hemisphere. Khartoum is warmer than Cape Juby throughout the year because it is nearer to the Equator. Cape Juby is almost as warm as Khartoum in January but is much cooler in summer due to the moderating influence of the sea. Coastal temperatures are also lowered in summer by a cold offshore ocean current (page 24). Away from the sea the cloudless skies of the central Sahara allow day time temperatures to reach 50°C, and night temperatures to drop to near freezing.

Rainfall

Although deserts, by definition, are dry, none are completely rainless. The lack of rain is due to several factors.

• Prevailing trade winds blow from the east and therefore across dry land.
• Prevailing winds have to cross mountain ranges so that most deserts lie in a rainshadow.
• Descending air at the Tropics warms (page 22), picks up moisture and creates areas of high pressure (page 14).
• When winds do blow from the sea they have to cross a cool surface and so cannot pick up much moisture.

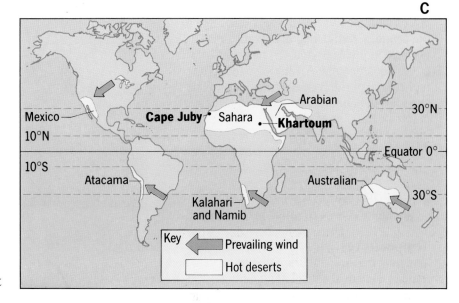

C

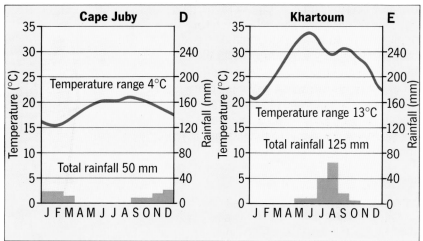

Khartoum gets most of its rain in summer when the overhead sun can trigger off occasional convectional downpours. Cape Juby gets a little rain in winter when the prevailing winds blow, for a short time, from the Atlantic Ocean and give some relief rainfall. Coastal areas also get fog when warm air from the land drifts out to sea to meet colder air.

Activities

1 a) Describe the location of those places with a hot desert climate.
   b) Name, with the help of an atlas, six countries which have a hot desert climate.
   c) Give four differences between the climate graph for Khartoum and a climate graph for a place in your home region.

2 a) Why do hot deserts have:
      i) high temperatures throughout the year?
      ii) very little rainfall?
   b) In hot deserts, why do coastal areas have lower summer temperatures and a higher annual temperature range than places which are inland?

Summary

Hot desert climates are usually located on the west coasts of continents between 15° and 30° north and south of the Equator. They are hot and dry throughout the year although coastal areas are much cooler than places which are inland.

▶ *Tropical continental (savanna) climates* ◀

Places with this type of climate are located in the centre of continents, approximately between latitudes 5° and 15° north and south of the Equator (map **A**). It is also found on the higher land of the East African plateau which straddles the Equator. Graph **B** is a climate graph for Kano in northern Nigeria. The climate has two distinct seasons.

1 A very warm, dry season when conditions are similar to those of the hot desert (page 19).
2 A hot, wet season when the weather more resembles that of equatorial areas (page 18).

Temperatures

Temperatures are high throughout the year and there is a relatively small annual range. The cooler, though not by British standards, season occurs when the sun is overhead in the opposite hemisphere. Temperatures rise as the angle of the sun in the sky increases (page 8), only to fall slightly at the time when there is most cloud and rainfall. Most areas are too far inland to be influenced by any moderating effect of the sea. Several places with this climate are in upland areas where temperatures are slightly reduced due to the increase in relief (altitude).

Rainfall

During the dry season the prevailing trade winds blow from the east. Any moisture which they carried will have been shed long before they reach the central parts of continents. The dry season is shorter towards the Equator and longer away from the Equator. The rainy season coincides with the time when the sun is overhead and the dry prevailing winds die away. The higher temperatures result in warm air being forced to rise to give frequent afternoon convectional thunderstorms (page 11). Unfortunately the length of the rainy season and the total amounts of rain are unreliable (page 23), while the heavy nature of the rain can cause more damage than good (page 26).

A

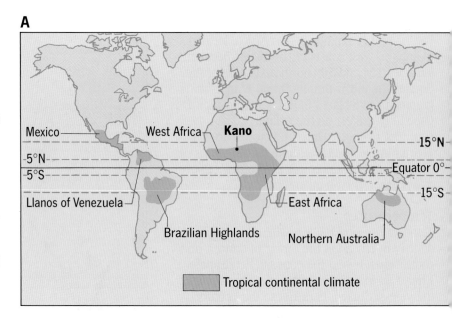

Mexico — West Africa — **Kano** — 15°N
5°N
5°S — Equator 0°
Llanos of Venezuela — East Africa — 15°S
Brazilian Highlands — Northern Australia

☐ Tropical continental climate

B

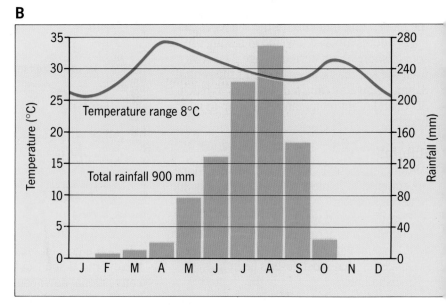

Temperature range 8°C

Total rainfall 900 mm

Activities

1 a) Describe the location of those places with a tropical continental climate.
   b) Name, with the help of an atlas, four countries which have a tropical continental climate.
   c) Give four differences between the climate graph for Kano and a climate graph for a place in your home region.

2 Why do tropical continental climates have:
   a) high temperatures throughout the year?
   b) a dry season and a wet season?

Summary

Tropical continental climates are usually located in the centre of continents between 5° and 15° north and south of the Equator. They have a very warm, dry season and a hot, wet season.

The Mediterranean climate

Places with a Mediterranean type of climate are located on west coasts of continents between latitudes 30° and 40° north and south of the Equator (map **C**). The exception is the area surrounding the 'inland' Mediterranean Sea. Graph **D** is a climate graph for Athens in Greece. The Mediterranean climate has two distinct seasons.

1 Hot, dry summers when the weather has similarities with that of the hot deserts (page 19).
2 Warm, wet winters when the weather more resembles that of the British Isles (page 6).

Temperatures

Temperatures can be very hot in summer. This is partly due to the sun being at a high, though never directly overhead, angle in the sky and partly because the prevailing trade winds blow from the warm land. Places on the extreme west coast are, however, cooler due to the moderating influence of the sea and the presence of a cold ocean current (page 24). Winters are warm partly due to the moderating influence of the sea and partly because of the prevailing winds which blow from the sea at this time of year. Many Mediterranean areas have high coastal mountains which lower temperatures considerably.

Rainfall

Summers often experience drought conditions due to the prevailing winds blowing from the dry land. Rain, when it does fall, often comes in short but heavy convectional thunderstorms. Winters can be very wet. This is due to the prevailing winds blowing from the sea and depressions moving eastwards which, together, give relief and frontal rain. Snow falls at higher altitudes.

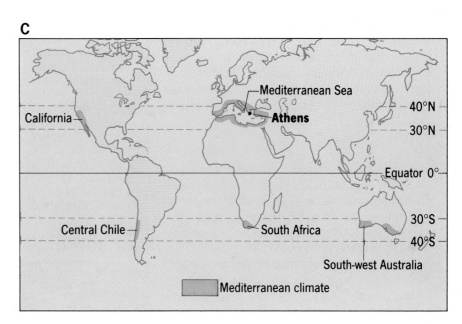

C

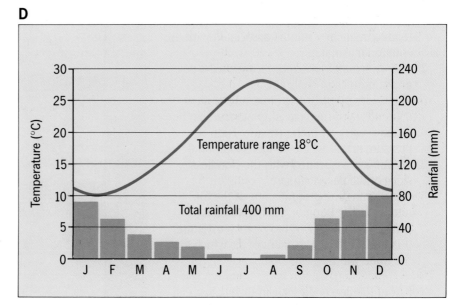

D

Activities

1 a) Describe the location of those places with a Mediterranean type of climate.
   b) Name, with the help of an atlas, six countries which have a Mediterranean climate.
   c) Give four differences between the climate graph for Athens and a climate graph for a place in your home region.

2 Why do Mediterranean climates have:
   a) hot, dry summers?
   b) warm, wet winters?

Summary

Mediterranean climates are usually located on west coasts of continents between 30° and 40° north and south of the Equator. Most places have hot, dry summers and warm, wet winters.

21

▶ *How does atmospheric circulation affect the pattern of world climates?* ◀

When describing the location of four of the world's types of climate (pages 18 to 21), it was pointed out that each type had a recognisable distribution pattern. This pattern results mainly from the circulation of air within the atmosphere. To understand **atmospheric circulation** you should be aware of three processes (table **A**).

The general circulation of the atmosphere is shown in diagram **B**. The diagram shows three circular movements, or **cells**, in each hemisphere. The most important cell, on a global scale, is the Hadley Cell. The cell consists of four segments.

1 With the sun always high in the sky, the ground on the Equator becomes very hot and water on the surface is evaporated. The hot air and water vapour rise in convection currents and an area of low pressure develops. As the rising air cools, it condenses to give the heavy rainfall associated with the equatorial climate.
2 The cooled air spreads out towards the poles and continues to cool.
3 The colder air begins to sink. As the air descends it warms, picks up moisture and forms an area of high pressure. High pressure areas, where condensation rarely occurs, are associated with the cloudless skies of the desert climate.
4 On reaching the ground some of the air returns to the Equator. As it does so it continues to warm and to pick up moisture. It is this surface movement of air which form the trade winds.

Not all of the descending air in the Hadley Cell returns to the Equator. Some of the warm, moist tropical air (in the northern hemisphere) travels northwards. This surface movement of air in the Ferrel Cell is the cause of Britain's prevailing south-westerly winds. Depressions form where the warm, moist tropical air meets the colder, drier air from the polar cell. The warm air is forced to rise over cold air to give the frontal rain and the frequent low pressure systems (depressions) which are characteristic of the British type of climate (page 11).

The location of the world's major types of climate does not, however, depend solely upon atmospheric circulation. Due to the tilt of the earth, the position of the overhead sun appears

A

1	When air next to the ground is heated, it expands, gets lighter and rises. As the amount of air next to the ground decreases, then an area of **low pressure** is formed.
2	When air in the atmosphere is cooled, it will become denser and heavier and so descends. As the amount of air next to the ground increases then an area of **high pressure** is formed.
3	Air will move, as wind, from areas of high pressure to areas of low pressure. However, air does not move directly from high to low. If it did then the direction of the prevailing winds in Britain would be from the south. Instead, due to factors such as the rotation of the earth, winds come from the south-west.

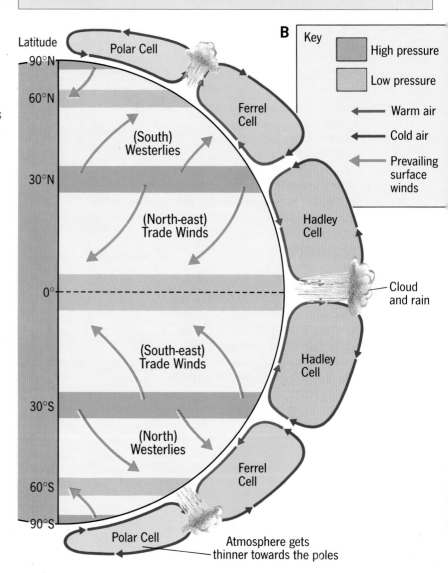

B

Key
- ▨ High pressure
- ▨ Low pressure
- ← Warm air
- ← Cold air
- ← Prevailing surface winds

Latitude
- 90°N — Polar Cell
- 60°N — Ferrel Cell
- (South) Westerlies
- 30°N — (North-east) Trade Winds — Hadley Cell
- 0° — Cloud and rain
- (South-east) Trade Winds — Hadley Cell
- 30°S — (North) Westerlies
- 60°S — Ferrel Cell
- 90°S — Polar Cell

Atmosphere gets thinner towards the poles

to change between seasons. On 21 June the sun is overhead at the Tropic of Cancer. As the sun 'appears' to move northwards, the equatorial low pressure belt moves several degrees north of the Equator. The result is that the prevailing wind belts, as shown on diagram **B** and map **D**, also move northwards. The reverse occurs on 21 December. At this time of the year the overhead sun, the equatorial low pressure, and the prevailing winds all move southwards. It is this seasonal change in pressure, and the resultant prevailing winds, which is responsible for the seasonal changes in the Mediterranean and tropical continental types of climate (diagram **C**).

The location of the four types of world climate described in this unit, together with that of the British type, are shown on map **D**. However, this map, like others which show the distribution of world climates, has to be interpreted with care!

- The map has been simplified, due to its scale, and so it cannot show local variations.
- The boundary between two climatic types is shown as a thin line. In reality the change between two adjacent climates is gradual and takes place over a wide area.

C

Climate type	Pressure	Prevailing winds	Rainfall
1 British type	Low all year all year	South-westerly all year	Frontal and relief
2 Mediterranean (transition between British type and hot desert)	Low in winter	South-westerly in winter	Frontal and relief in winter
	High in summer	North-east trades in summer	Very little
3 Hot deserts	High all year	North-east trades all year	Very little
4 Tropical continental (transitional between hot desert and equatorial)	High in winter	North-east trades in 'winter'	Very little
	Low in 'summer'	None in 'summer'	Convectional rain
5 Equatorial	Low all year	None	Convectional all year

Key **D**

- Low pressure
- High pressure
- → Prevailing winds

Climate types
- Equatorial
- Hot desert
- Tropical continental
- Mediterranean
- British

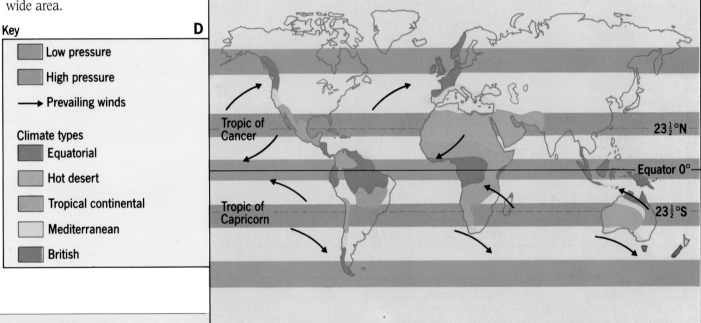

Tropic of Cancer · *Tropic of Capricorn* · 23½°N · Equator 0° · 23½°S

Activities

1 Explain how areas of low pressure and areas of high pressure are formed.

2 Diagram **E** shows the two Hadley Cells, one either side of the Equator.
 a) Copy the diagram and add eight arrow heads to show the direction of air movement.
 b) Label the three boxes either 'high pressure' or 'low pressure'.
 c) Briefly describe the differences in climate between an area with low pressure all the year and an area with high pressure all the year.

E

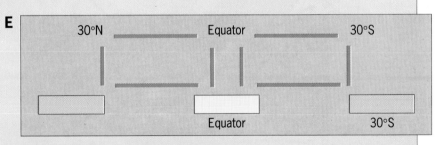

30°N — Equator — 30°S

Equator · 30°S

3 Explain how atmospheric circulation influences the climate of the British Isles.

Summary The general circulation of the atmosphere is the main factor affecting the world pattern of climatic types.

23

▶ How do ocean currents affect the climate of coastal areas? ◀

Ocean currents are surface movements of water. They are caused by prevailing winds, which result from the circulation of the atmosphere, blowing over the surface of the ocean (map **A**). The main ocean currents follow circular routes - clockwise in the northern hemisphere and anti-clockwise in the southern hemisphere (map **B**).

Ocean currents often flow parallel to the coastlines of continents. Where they do, they usually have a considerable influence upon the climate of those coasts. Exactly how ocean currents influence the climate depends largely upon whether the current is warm or cold. Warm currents take water from tropical areas towards polar areas, e.g. the North

Atlantic Drift. They are described as warm because they raise the temperatures of coastal areas making them warmer than would be expected for their latitude. In contrast, cold currents take water from colder latitudes back towards the Equator, e.g. the Californian Current. Consequently they lower the temperatures of coastal areas.

Newfoundland and the British Isles lie in approximately the same latitude. However, while the seas off Newfoundland are frozen for several months each winter, the North Atlantic Drift keeps Britain ice-free. Even so, anybody falling into the sea off the west coast of Britain in winter is unlikely to survive if left in the water for more than a few minutes!

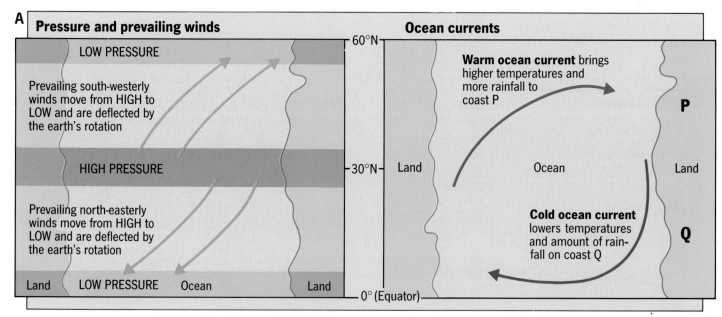

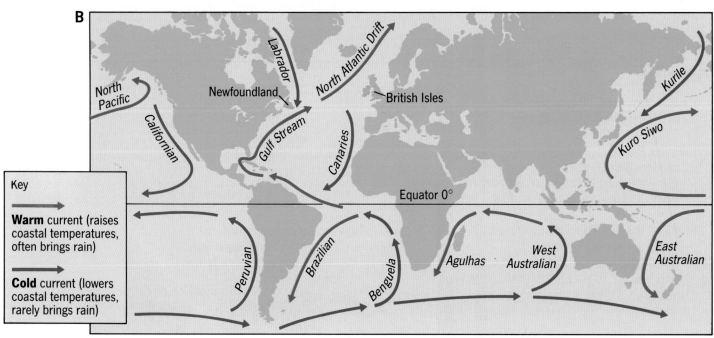

Table **C** describes and explains how two contrasting ocean currents, the warm North Atlantic Drift and the cold Californian Current, have very different influences upon the coastal climates of areas which they affect.

C

Type of current	Location	Source and direction of current	Effects on temperature	Effects on precipitation	Other climatic effects
Warm	Influence of North Atlantic Drift on the climate of the British Isles.	Begins in Caribbean Sea and Gulf of Mexico. Flows up east coast of USA as the Gulf Stream, then north-east across Atlantic Ocean.	Raises them in winter by several degrees – mild. Lowers them in summer – cool.	Allows much moisture to be picked up. This gives heavy and reliable rainfall throughout the year.	Warm air meets cold air to form depressions and to give strong winds (i.e. gales).
Cold	Influence of the Californian Current on the climate of California.	Begins off west coast of Canada and flows southwards.	Lowers them in summer by several degrees – relatively cool. Raises them a little in winter – warm.	Prevents moisture from being picked up. Gives little rainfall and adds to desert conditions to south.	Warm air drifts out to sea over cold air to give fogs.

Activities

1 a) What are ocean currents?
  b) With the help of an annotated diagram, explain how the pattern of ocean currents in the Atlantic Ocean is related to prevailing winds.

2 Diagram **D** shows part of an ocean which lies north of the Equator.
  a) Are the currents flowing clockwise or anti-clockwise?
  b) Is current **A** a warm or a cold current? Give a reason for your answer.
  c) Is current **B** a warm or a cold current? Give a reason for your answer.
  d) Make an enlarged copy of table **E**. Complete it to show likely differences in the climate between places **X** and **Y** which are located on the same coast of a large continent.

D

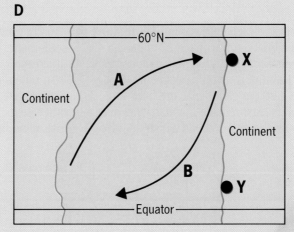

E

Place	Temperatures		Precipitation	
	Summer	Winter	Amounts	Type
X				
Y				

Summary

The global pattern of ocean currents is related to prevailing winds and the general circulation of the atmosphere. Ocean currents have a major influence upon the climates of adjacent coastal areas.

▶ Why is rainfall unreliable in some parts of the world? ◀

Rainfall in the British Isles is reliable. We know that in a usual year it will rain every few days, rainfall will be spread evenly throughout the twelve months, and that the total amount for each place can be fairly accurately predicted. Occasionally some seasons are wetter and others drier than is expected, but annual totals are nearly always within 10 per cent of the expected average total (map **A**). The driest summer ever recorded in England and Wales was in 1976. It caused a serious drought. Yet it was followed by the second wettest winter ever recorded and so, over a twelve month period, rainfall virtually averaged itself out.

Not only is rainfall reliable in Britain, but so too is water supply. When it does rain it usually falls steadily for a period of several hours. This allows time for the water to infiltrate into the ground where it can be stored for use in drier periods. The British Isles rarely get the severe storms which cause rapid surface run-off and flash floods. Britain also has the capital and technology to build dams so that surplus water can be stored in reservoirs and then piped to where and when it is needed. On a global scale, many countries still do not have a guaranteed supply 'at the turn of a tap'.

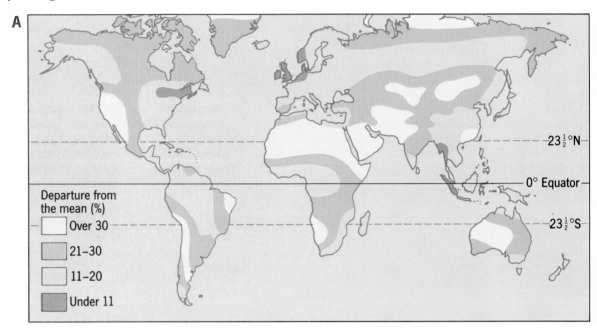

A

Departure from the mean (%)

Over 30

21–30

11–20

Under 11

$23\frac{1}{2}°$N

$0°$ Equator

$23\frac{1}{2}°$S

There is a relationship between reliability of rainfall (map **A**), the pattern of world climatic types (page 23) and the circulation of the atmosphere (page 22). This relationship is summarised in table **B**. Rainfall is usually reliable in places where there is less than a 20 per cent departure from the mean (average). Rainfall is least reliable in areas with over a 30 per cent departure from the mean, areas which are also

usually either too dry or too cold for permanent human settlement. It is those climates with a pronounced wet and dry season, especially in tropical continental areas (page 20), where rainfall is most unreliable in relation to human activity. Here, in some years, the rains may fail to arrive. In other years, when it does rain, total amounts can come from just a few heavy storms. The rain will then be too heavy to

B

Departure from the mean (%)	Atmospheric pressure	Vertical air movement	Surface prevailing winds	Rainfall distribution	Effectiveness of rain
Under 20	Low (i) Equatorial (ii) British type	Rising air cools, condenses and gives rain	Equatorial – none British type – south-west from the sea	Throughout the year	Equatorial – heavy but intercepted by vegetation Britain – steady
20-30	Seasonal – tropical continental	Rising air giving rain for part of the year. Descending air giving no rain for rest of year	Either too far inland or dry trade winds	Wet season and a dry season	Heavy storms; little interception; less effective and much surface run-off
Over 30	High (i) Hot desert (ii) Polar	Descending air warms, so no condensation	Trade winds from dry land	Very little	Ineffective – short, intense storms

allow infiltration and so the precious water is lost through surface run-off and flash floods. As the rainy season coincides with the time of highest temperatures then evaporation rates, and therefore water loss, will also be at their greatest. Drought frequently occurs in countries along the southern fringes of the Sahara Desert when annual rainfall totals fall below average for several successive years. Unreliable rainfall is one of several important reasons why so many countries with a tropical continental climate, especially in Africa, have remained economically less developed. This creates a vicious circle since, because they are economically less developed, they have less capital and technology to improve their water supply.

Diagram **C** gives some of the consequences of unreliable rainfall upon human activity in Kenya. In a normal year it is estimated that Kenya receives enough rainfall, if it was spread out evenly, to sustain a population several times greater than it has at present. Unfortunately the distribution of rainfall and population does not always match, and rainfall is not always reliable.

C

Maasai herder
We depend upon our cattle, sheep and goats. When the rains fail, there is overgrazing and eventually our animals will die.

Industrialist
We need energy to manufacture goods. We have to rely upon hydro-electricity. If the rains fail, reservoirs dry up and the power stations have to close down. We had big power cuts in Nairobi in 1992.

Wildlife worker
Drought also kills wildlife. In the 1970s thousands of elephants died.

Villager
We have no piped water. If the rains fail, rivers and waterholes dry up and we may have to walk many miles to get water.

Farmer
We need water for our crops. We need more crops since our population is growing so rapidly. If the rains do not come at the right time, and in sufficient quantity, our crops will fail and we shall be short of food.

Government official
Kenya is an economically developing country. We do not have enough money to build dams to store water for times of drought. We have several dams but not enough. One big dam was built for us using French money but that accounts for two-thirds of our national debt.

Activities

1 Give three reasons why rainfall in the British Isles is reliable.

2 a) Write out the paragraph below using the correct word from each pair in brackets.

Rainfall is most unreliable in areas with (high/low) pressure, when air is (descending/rising) and (cooling/warming), where winds blow from the (land/sea), and when it falls in (long/short) (storms/periods).

b) Which two of the following four climates have the least reliable rainfall:
• equatorial   • tropical continental
• hot deserts   • British type?

3 a) How does an unreliable water supply affect a country such as Kenya?

b) Do you agree or disagree with the statement made in diagram **D**? Give reasons for your answer.

D
The most serious single climatic hazard in an economically less developed country is the variability and uncertainty of rainfall

Summary

The distribution of areas with a markedly unreliable rainfall can be related to the general pattern of atmospheric circulation and to specific climatic types.

What are the causes and effects of global warming?

Heat from the sun passes through the atmosphere. During the day this heat warms up the surface of the earth. On clear nights, much of this heat is lost (radiated) back into space and temperatures fall rapidly. On cloudy nights temperatures do not fall as low because the clouds act as a blanket retaining some of the heat. The atmosphere consists of various gases, of which oxygen and nitrogen make up 99 per cent. The remaining 1 per cent includes variable amounts of the two natural gases of carbon dioxide and ozone, and pollutants such as methane, sulphur dioxide and nitrogen oxide. It is changes in the amounts of these variable gases and pollutants which are causing concern to scientists.

Carbon dioxide is important because its helps to trap heat. The ability of this, and other, gases to insulate the earth is referred to as the **greenhouse effect**. The natural greenhouse effect is essential as without it the earth's average temperature would be 33°C lower than it is. (During the last Ice Age temperatures were only 4°C lower than they are today). Recent human activity has led to an increase in greenhouse gases. This is causing world temperatures to rise, a process known as **global warming** (diagram **A**).

Causes

Graph **B** shows the major causes of global warming. The most important single factor has been the burning of fossil fuels in power stations, factories, homes and by road transport. As it is the economically more developed and industrialised countries which use up most of the world's energy, then they are largely to blame for global warming (graph **C**). A second cause is deforestation (pages 38–43), especially the burning of the tropical rainforests in economically developing countries.

Consequences

Although global warming results mainly from activities within relatively few countries, its consequences affect all parts of the world. Indeed, it is likely that its effects will be greatest in many countries which, at present, are not major contributors to greenhouse gas emissions. This is because gases released into the air, and the resultant rise in temperature, do not stop at national boundaries. Global temperatures have risen by 0.5°C in the last 100 years. Estimates suggest that, without controls on greenhouse gas emissions, temperatures could rise by up to 0.5°C each decade over the next 100 years (graph **D**). The major global effect is the predicted rise in world sea-level. Scientists are suggesting that as air temperatures rise then

- sea temperatures will also rise. As the sea expands, due to the extra heat, its level could rise by between 0.25 and 1.5 metres.
- ice caps and glaciers, especially in polar areas, will melt. This could result in an overall rise in sea-level by up to another 5 metres.

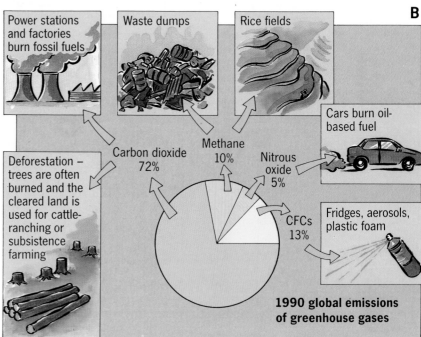

The greenhouse effect
Carbon dioxide level is increased by burning fossil fuels and cutting down forests

Carbon dioxide in atmosphere

Some heat escapes

Sun's heat

Less heat escapes

Carbon dioxide traps heat being reflected by the earth

Warming increases water vapour in air

A

Power stations and factories burn fossil fuels

Waste dumps

Rice fields

Cars burn oil-based fuel

Deforestation – trees are often burned and the cleared land is used for cattle-ranching or subsistence farming

Carbon dioxide 72%

Methane 10%

Nitrous oxide 5%

CFCs 13%

Fridges, aerosols, plastic foam

1990 global emissions of greenhouse gases

B

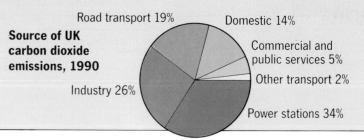

Source of UK carbon dioxide emissions, 1990

Road transport 19%

Domestic 14%

Commercial and public services 5%

Other transport 2%

Power stations 34%

Industry 26%

Even a half metre rise in sea-level could flood 15 per cent of densely populated Bangladesh, 25 per cent of Egypt's arable land, and submerge several lowlying islands in the Indian and Pacific Oceans (map **E**).

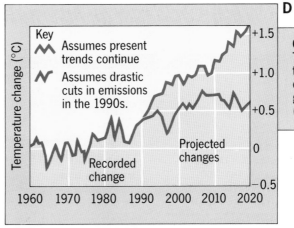

D

Global warming
The rise in average temperatures caused by carbon dioxide and other greenhouse gases (1960–2020)

C

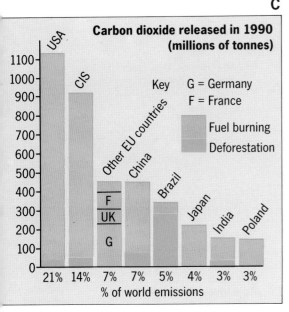

Carbon dioxide released in 1990 (millions of tonnes)

Other predicted effects of global warming include an increase in storms and hurricanes in tropical areas and a decrease in rainfall in most of the world's major cereal growing areas. The latter would result from air being able to hold more moisture as it gets warmer. As a result there will be a decrease in rainfall totals and an increase in its unreliability (page 26).

Gaining international agreement to reduce the releases of greenhouse gases, especially carbon dioxide, is difficult. Industrialised countries are reluctant, claiming that the high economic costs involved could cause job losses and a lowering of their standards of living. Developing countries are reluctant, believing that they need to increase consumption if they are to create new jobs and raise their living standards. They also fail to see why they should help to solve a problem which they did not create.

E

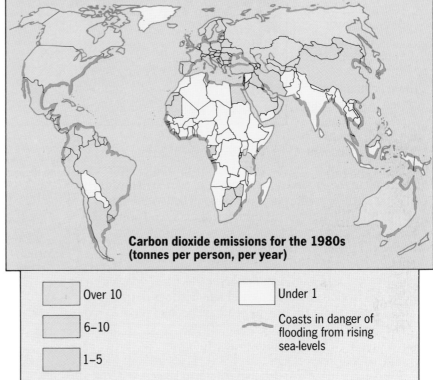

Carbon dioxide emissions for the 1980s (tonnes per person, per year)

Over 10

6–10

1–5

Under 1

Coasts in danger of flooding from rising sea-levels

Activities

1 a) Draw a labelled diagram to explain the greenhouse effect.
   b) i) What are the four main greenhouse gases?
      ii) What is the source of each of these four greenhouse gases?
   c) Which countries contribute most to the greenhouse effect?

2 a) How is global warming predicted to affect the world's
      i) temperatures
      ii) sea-level
      iii) cereal production?
   b) i) Why is international agreement on the reduction of greenhouse gases necessary?
      ii) Why is it difficult to get this international agreement?

Summary

Global warming is caused by an increase in the emission of greenhouse gases, especially carbon dioxide, by a relatively few industrialised countries. As the consequences will affect the whole world, there is a need for international co-operation and agreement.

▶ *Why is acid rain an international problem?* ◀

Acid rain, resulting from air pollution, has become a major global environmental problem. The main air pollutants are:

- sulphur dioxide which comes from thermal power stations and industry.
- nitrogen oxide which comes from thermal power stations and motor vehicle exhausts.

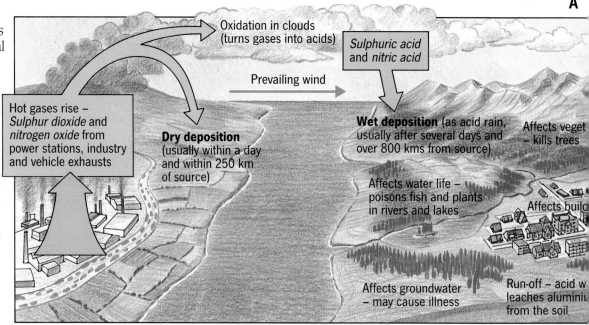

A

Oxidation in clouds (turns gases into acids)

Sulphuric acid and *nitric acid*

Prevailing wind

Hot gases rise – *Sulphur dioxide* and *nitrogen oxide* from power stations, industry and vehicle exhausts

Dry deposition (usually within a day and within 250 km of source)

Wet deposition (as acid rain, usually after several days and over 800 kms from source)

Affects veget – kills trees

Affects water life – poisons fish and plants in rivers and lakes

Affects buil

Affects groundwater – may cause illness

Run-off – acid w leaches alumini from the soil

These pollutants are carried by prevailing winds across seas and international boundaries (diagram **A**). Some are deposited directly onto the earth's surface. The majority are converted into acids which fall to the ground as acid rain. Unpolluted rainwater, which is slightly acidic, has a pH value of between 5 and 6 (graph **B**). Acid rain has pH readings of under 5. Parts of North-east North America and North-west Europe have readings of under 4.0 (map **C**).

The effects of acid rain (diagram **A)** include:

- the destruction of forests as acid rain destroys tree roots (photo **D**). The trees are then more likely to suffer from drought and disease.
- Making fresh water lakes so acidic that fish and plant life is poisoned. Over 4000 lakes in Sweden are 'dead'. British and Canadian lakes are also becoming increasingly affected.
- Contaminating fresh water supplies which might, in time, become harmful to health.
- Increasing the acidity of soil which, unless lime is added, reduces the quality of crops.
- The chemical weathering of buildings and statues (photo **E**).

Acid rain is an international problem because it is blown across oceans and continents ignoring political boundaries. Many countries produce acid rain (map **C**). Some, like Britain, Germany and the USA, 'export' it while others, such as Norway, Sweden and Canada, 'import' it. Any solution to the problem requires international co-operation. This is not easy as the countries most affected by acid rain are often not the same ones that are responsible for causing it.

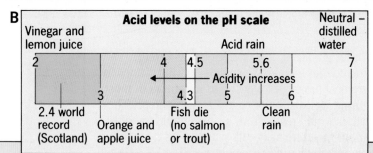

B

Acid levels on the pH scale

Vinegar and lemon juice

Acid rain

Neutral – distilled water

2   4   4.5   5.6   7

Acidity increases ◀

3   4.3   5   6

2.4 world record (Scotland)

Orange and apple juice

Fish die (no salmon or trout)

Clean rain

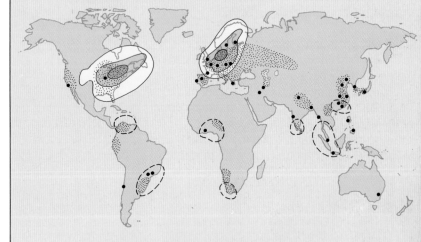

C

Regions where sulphur and nitrogen oxides are released in high concentrations, mainly from burning fossil fuels

Areas where acid rain is a potential danger

• Major cities with high levels of air pollution (including nitrogen and sulphur emissions)

Areas of heavy acid deposition

pH less than 4 (most acidic)

pH 4 to 4.5

pH 4.6 to 5

How might the effects of acid rain be reduced?

There are several ways by which sulphur dioxide emissions from power stations may be reduced. These include burning coal which contains less sulphur, removing sulphur from coal before it is used, using a new type of boiler which allows the sulphur dioxide to remain in the ash, and removing sulphur from waste gases after it is used. The latter method involves spraying sulphur dioxide with water. This converts the gas into sulphuric acid which can then be neutralised by adding lime. Unfortunately all of these methods are expensive and increase the cost of electricity to the user. Britain is committed to reducing sulphur dioxide emissions by 60 per cent of their 1980 levels by the year 2000 and 71 per cent by 2005. So far they have been reduced by 30 per cent. Some European countries say this is too little and is taking too long, but it has been achieved by phasing out coal-burning power stations in favour of cheaper gas-fired stations. This phasing out has accelerated the decline of Britain's coal mining industry as the demand for coal falls.

Emissions from cars have been reduced by using unleaded petrol and fuel injection. Further attempts, such as recirculating exhaust gases, are likely to add to the cost of a new car.

D Acid rain damage to trees, Poland

E
The effects of acid rain on Lincoln Cathedral

Activities

1 a) What is acid rain?
  b) What, according to graph **F**, are the two major producers of
    i) sulphur dioxide,
    ii) nitrogen oxide?
  c) Describe five problems caused by acid rain.

2 Refer to map **C**.
  a) Describe the location of the major concentrations of sulphur and nitrogen oxides.
  b) i) Why do countries like Norway, Sweden and Canada want rapid decreases in the emissions of sulphur and nitrogen oxides?
    ii) Why are countries like Britain, Germany and the USA reluctant to reduce these emissions?

3 Two views are expressed in diagram **G**. Which of these views is likely to be supported by
  i) an industrialist,
  ii) a coal-miner,
  iii) a conservationist?
  Give reasons, in each case, for your answer.

F

Sulphur dioxide

0   20   40   60   80   100%

Nitrogen oxide

Key

Power stations   Industry   Domestic   Transport

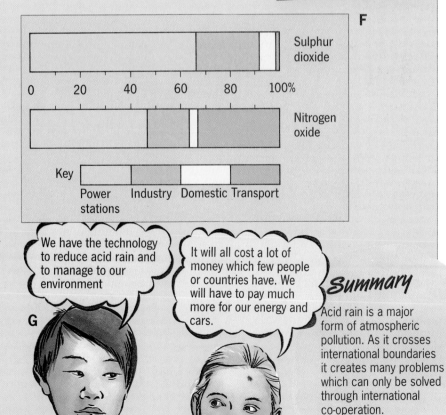

We have the technology to reduce acid rain and to manage to our environment

It will all cost a lot of money which few people or countries have. We will have to pay much more for our energy and cars.

G

Summary

Acid rain is a major form of atmospheric pollution. As it crosses international boundaries it creates many problems which can only be solved through international co-operation.

▶ What are the characteristics of the tropical rainforests? ◀

Tropical rainforest is the natural vegetation of places which have an equatorial climate (page 18). They provide the most luxuriant vegetation found on earth (photos **B** and **C**). Over one-third of the world's trees grow here. There are thousands of different species and many have yet to be identified and studied. As with all types of natural vegetation, the trees in the rainforest have had to **adapt** to the local environment. This means that, here they have had to adjust to growing in a climate which has constantly high temperatures and heavy rainfall, and an all year round growing season. Some of the ways in which the trees have adapted to the climate are shown in diagram **A**. The vegetation has also had to adapt to other local conditions such as soils, flooding and competition from other plants. Different plants also survive in their own micro-climate (page 9), perhaps as an emergent needing to reach the sunlight, perhaps as a shade-lover on the forest floor. Each plant plays an important role in the forest ecosystem.

A

Height of trees which grow in **three layers**

40 m

Tallest trees called **emergents**

30 m

CANOPY

20 m

UNDER CANOPY

Lianas

10 m

Buttress roots

SHRUB LAYER

Ground level

How vegetation has adapted to the equatorial climate

- The trees can grow to over 40 metres in the effort to get sunlight

- The forest has an **evergreen** appearance due to the continuous growing season. This means that trees can shed leaves at any time, but always look green and in leaf

- The leaves have drip tips to shed the heavy rainfall

- Tree trunks are straight and branchless in their lower parts in their efforts to grow tall

- Lianas, which are vine-like plants, use large trees as a support to climb up to the canopy

- The forest floor is dark and damp. There is little undergrowth because the sunlight cannot reach ground level

- Dense undergrowth develops near rivers or in forest clearings where sunlight can penetrate

- Rivers flood for several months each year

- Fallen leaves soon rot in the hot, wet climate

- Large buttress roots stand above the ground to give support to the trees

B Aerial view of the Korup National Park, Cameroon

C Ground view of the rainforest showing layers of vegetation

Until recently few parts of the rainforest had been affected by human activity. Where it had, it was usually by groups of people clearing just enough land on which to grow crops for their small community. Often, in places like the Amazon forest, the land rapidly became infertile and the people had to move and make a new clearing. This method of farming, known as shifting cultivation, allowed the forest to re-establish itself. Re-established areas often have a thicker undergrowth as the initial clearance allowed more sunlight to reach the forest floor. More recently, increased human activity has led to vast areas of the rainforest being totally destroyed, a process known as **deforestation** (page 38). As large trees are destroyed, the habitat for other plants and wildlife will be altered. Plants which cannot adapt quickly to the changed environment may die out.

Activities

1 Match up each of the eight descriptive points of the tropical rainforest from the list below with its correct number on diagram **D**.
   buttress roots • main canopy • lianas • under-canopy • branchless trunks • little undergrowth • emergents • shrub layer

2 a) Why does rainforest vegetation grow so quickly?
   b) Why do some trees grow so tall?
   c) Why are buttress roots needed?
   d) Why is there so little undergrowth away from the rivers?

3 a) Why did earlier human activity have little effect upon the tropical rainforest vegetation?
   b) Why are present day human actions having a far greater effect?

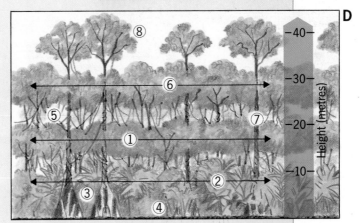

D

Summary   The natural vegetation of the tropical rainforest has had to adapt to the hot, wet equatorial climate. It is now being increasingly affected by human activity.

▶ *What are the characteristics of the savanna grassland vegetation?* ◀

The savanna grassland, which often includes scattered trees (photos **B** and **C**), is the natural vegetation of places with a tropical continental climate (page 20). The vegetation forms a transition between the tropical rainforests and the hot deserts (map **D**, page 23). As with all types of natural vegetation the plants growing here have had to **adapt** to the local environment. This means that they have had to adjust to a very warm climate which has a pronounced wet season, though the rainfall is often unreliable (page 26), followed by a very long dry season. Some of the ways in which the grass and trees have adapted to the climate are shown in diagram **A**. Apart from the major problem of water supply caused by the seasonal drought, the vegetation has also had to adapt to other local conditions such as soils, relief and competition from other plants.

A

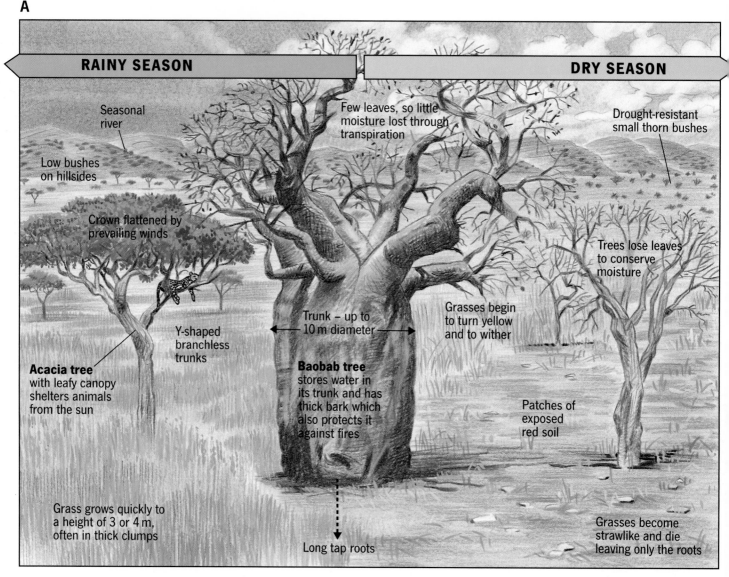

RAINY SEASON

DRY SEASON

Seasonal river

Low bushes on hillsides

Crown flattened by prevailing winds

Acacia tree with leafy canopy shelters animals from the sun

Y-shaped branchless trunks

Grass grows quickly to a height of 3 or 4 m, often in thick clumps

Few leaves, so little moisture lost through transpiration

Trunk – up to 10 m diameter

Baobab tree stores water in its trunk and has thick bark which also protects it against fires

Long tap roots

Drought-resistant small thorn bushes

Trees lose leaves to conserve moisture

Grasses begin to turn yellow and to wither

Patches of exposed red soil

Grasses become strawlike and die leaving only the roots

It has been suggested that the savanna grasses are not the natural vegetation of tropical continental climates. Rather they are the result of fires started either naturally or by human activity. Fires can result from either:
- lightning associated with convectional thunderstorms in the rainy season or
- by cattle herders burning off the old grass during the dry season to encourage new shoots to sprout when the rains come.

The thick bark of the baobab tree (photo **B**) acts as a protection against fires.

B
Baobab tree

Recently many parts of the savanna grasslands, especially in Africa, which are near to the desert margins have suffered from drought and **desertification** (pages 48-49). The unreliable rainfall has caused vegetation to die. With insufficient grass for the large herds of wild and domestic grazing animals, the area suffers from **overgrazing** (page 49). As the human population increases former nomadic tribes, like the Maasai in Kenya, find their traditional grazing grounds reduced in size as the land becomes settled permanently or is used to grow crops. This too causes overgrazing in the areas to which they are restricted. The increase in the human population has also meant that more trees and shrubs are cut for fuelwood or to create extra land for crops. With fewer trees and less grass to protect the land from the weather, the soil may be washed away during the rainy season or blown away during the dry season.

C
Acacia trees on the savanna grassland

Activities

1 Photo **C** was taken during the rainy season.
   a) Describe the appearance of the natural vegetation of the savanna grasslands during the rainy season.
   b) What differences will there be in the appearance of the natural vegetation during the dry season?
   c) Draw a baobab tree similar to the one shown in photo **B**. Add at least four labels to show how the tree has adapted to the climate.

2 Diagram **D** shows how the natural vegetation of parts of the savanna grassland is being changed.
   a) Name three changes which are natural (not the result of human activity).
   b) Name four changes which are the result of human activity.
   c) Describe how these changes are altering the natural vegetation of the savanna grasslands.

Summary

The natural vegetation of the savanna grassland has had to adapt to a warm climate which has a wet and a dry season. It is being increasingly affected by human activity.

D

Drought for several years

Thunderstorm

Maasai herders

New houses

Collecting fuelwood

Herds of domestic cattle and goats

Large herds of wildebeeste, zebra and other wild herbivores

Newly planted maize

▶ *What are the characteristics of Mediterranean vegetation?* ◀

Mediterranean woodland and scrub (photos **B** and **C**) is the natural vegetation of places which have a Mediterranean type of climate (page 21). As with all types of natural vegetation, the plants which grow here have had to **adapt** to the local environment. This means that, here, they have had to adjust to a climate which has hot, dry summers and mild, wet winters. Some of the ways by which the trees and shrubs have adapted to the climate are shown in diagram **A**. The vegetation has also had to adapt to other local conditions such as soils, relief, different rock types and competition from other plants.

The natural vegetation of the Mediterranean lands in Europe was woodland. Where this still exists the main trees are often evergreen oaks and pines (e.g. cork oak and Corsican pine). Where the woodland has been cut down, it has been succeeded by one of two types of scrub.

- Maquis is a dense tangle of undergrowth and grows on granite and other impermeable rocks.
- Garrigue is a less dense and lower lying scrub which includes many aromatic plants such as rosemary and lavender. It develops on limestone and other permeable rocks.

A

Pine

Cypress

Cork oak

Some have thick bark as protection against the heat

Many have small, thin, waxy or leathery leaves to reduce moisture loss

LOW SCRUB

Sweet-smelling herbs

Rosemary

Lavender

Thyme

Very little grass. Too hot and too dry.

Quick life cycle to fit into the short growing season

Many plants have long roots to reach down to underground water

Rosemary can roll its leaves up tightly to reduce moisture loss

Due to human activities over many centuries, little of the natural Mediterranean woodland survives today. It has been changed as a result of:

- **Deforestation** Some of the earliest civilisations and empires (Greek and Roman) grew up on the shores of the Mediterranean Sea. Their inhabitants cleared many of the natural forests. They needed the space for farming and for settlement. Wood was needed for the construction of ships, the building of houses, and as a fuel for bothcooking and warmth. Deforestation left the many steep mountainsides vulnerable to soil erosion during the heavy winter rains.
- **Grazing animals** Forests were unable to re-establish themselves as herds of sheep and, especially, goats ate the young shoots.
- **Fire** Forest fires were, and still are, extremely dangerous. The fires, often started deliberately during the long, dry summers, have added to the destruction of the forests and, more recently, human property.

B Mediterranean woodland

C Mediterranean scrub

D

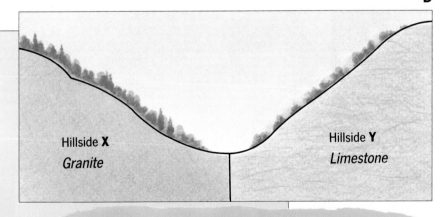

Hillside **X**
Granite

Hillside **Y**
Limestone

Activities

1 Draw a simple diagram of a named Mediterranean tree (diagram **A**). Add three labels to show how it has adapted to the summer drought.

2 Using diagram **D**, describe the type of vegetation likely to grow on
   a) hillside **X**,
   b) hillside **Y**.

3 Describe three different human activities which have changed the natural vegetation of those places surrounding the Mediterranean Sea.

Summary The natural vegetation of places with a Mediterranean climate has had to adapt to a climate which has hot, dry summers and warm, wet winters. In countries surrounding the Mediterranean Sea, the vegetation has been changed over many centuries by human activity.

▶ Deforestation – why are the rainforests being cleared? ◀

Deforestation is the felling and clearance of forest land. Deforestation began in the Mediterranean lands (page 37) and North-west Europe many centuries ago. Today it is mainly taking place in those economically less developed countries which have tropical rainforests as their natural vegetation (page 33). The rapid clearances in recent years has made deforestation a key global environmental issue. Some estimates suggest that one-fifth of the Amazon forest was cleared between 1960 and 1990 (map **A**). Whereas in 1980 an area the size of Wales was cleared, by 1990 the cleared area had increased more to the size of Great Britain (i.e. one hectare cleared every two seconds). The fastest clearances are still taking place in Brazil (graph **B**). Satellite photographs have shown that, on occasions, up to 5000 individual fires may be burning at the same time. These fires release carbon dioxide and smoke which pollute the atmosphere and reduce visibility (photo **C**). Although the rainforests 'may provide the most luxuriant vegetation found on earth' (page 32), they are still a fragile environment which, once destroyed, are unlikely to be replaced.

A

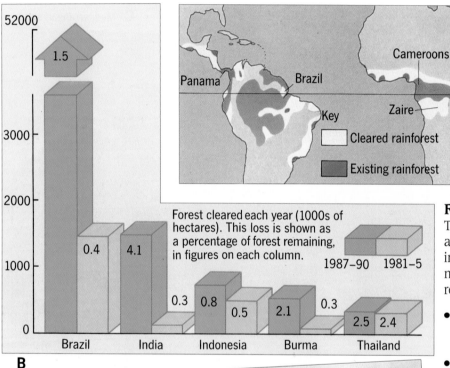

B

Forest cleared each year (1000s of hectares). This loss is shown as a percentage of forest remaining, in figures on each column.

1987–90   1981–5

Brazil: 1.5, 0.4, 4.1
India: 0.3, 0.8
Indonesia: 0.5, 2.1
Burma: 0.3
Thailand: 2.5, 2.4

Reasons for clearances

The earth's remaining rainforests are under attack by a rapidly growing population, and an increasing demand by that population for natural resources. Deforestation can be the result of several types of activity (diagram **D**).

- Government policy, such as in Brazil where attempts have been made to resettle some of the country's many landless people.
- Multinational companies, which wish to grow cash crops, extract raw materials or develop energy on a commercial scale.
- Local people, who need more land on which to grow crops if they are to be able to feed themselves.

By 1990 plans had been made for a wide range of developments which would affect over 60 per cent of Brazil's remaining rainforest. At that same time, less than 4 per cent of Brazil's rainforest was protected from development by law.

C Amazon rainforest being burned for cattle ranching

D

Causes of deforestation in Brazil

Most clearances are still by local people and tribes needing land on which to grow crops. We clear the forest by 'slash and burn'. We often leave an area after five years to let the ground recover.

Sometimes the natural forest is cleared and replanted, often with a single crop. These 'plantations' (rubber, sugar, coffee) are often owned by big companies.

There are nearly three million landless people in Brazil. The government has cleared large areas of forest and encouraged people like me to move there. We were encouraged to set up small farms on land that we were able to buy cheaply.

The mining of iron ore, bauxite, gold and other minerals, and the building of hydro-electric power stations have benefited the country. They have also destroyed large areas of forest.

Many economically less developed countries have rapidly growing populations. More people means that more food is needed. Forest is cleared for growing crops.

The economically more developed countries want our timber and we need their money. Logging is the second largest cause of deforestation. Unfortunately when large trees are felled they often pull down many nearby trees with them.

Multinational companies have bought large areas of forest which they have turned into huge cattle ranches. Two-thirds of the forests of central America now raise cattle which produce meat for economically more developed countries.

Many roads, such as the Trans-Amazonia Highway, have been built to try to develop the centre of Brazil. They are needed to move timber, cattle, minerals and export crops. People from poor areas have been settled along these main roads.

Activities

1 a) What is deforestation?
   b) Which parts of the world are experiencing most deforestation?
   c) Why is rapid deforestation taking place in those parts of the world?

2 a) Give eight reasons why the tropical rainforests are being cleared in countries like Brazil.
   b) Which of those reasons benefit
      i) local people,
      ii) Brazil's government,
      iii) multinational companies?

Summary

The effects of population growth and economic development have always put pressure on natural resources, especially forests. Today it is the tropical rainforests where deforestation is greatest.

Deforestation - what are the consequences?

Loss of wildlife

Many birds, insects, reptiles and animals rely upon the trees for food or shelter. They die or are forced to move away if their habitat is destroyed.

Loss of medicines

Over half of our modern medicines come from the rainforests. These include painkillers and quinine (used to treat malaria). Recently one plant, a periwinkle, has proved successful in treating child leukaemia. Perhaps the rainforests may hold cures for cancer and AIDS. If they are cleared, we shall never know!

Elimination of Indian groups and their way of life

Estimates suggest 96 per cent of forest Indians have died since the arrival of Europeans in the sixteenth century. The majority have died from western illnesses to which they had no immunity (e.g. measles, influenza). Those remaining have been driven from their homes by the construction of roads, mines, reservoirs and cattle ranches (photo **A**). They have been forced to live on reservations which have few natural resources, and certainly none that are of value to the developers. In several parts of Brazil, Indians who have tried to resist being moved have been killed by developers.

Soil erosion

The forest canopy protects the soil by intercepting the heavy daily convectional rainfall. The tree roots help to bind the soil together and to reduce throughflow. Without the trees there is increased surface run-off which causes both soil erosion and more severe and frequent flooding.

Decrease in soil fertility

In order to live, trees take nutrients from the soil. Dead trees, and leaves shed from trees, rapidly decompose in the hot, wet climate. This allows the nutrients to be returned to the soil. This process is called the **humus**, or **nutrient**, **cycle** (diagram **B**). If trees are removed then the cycle is broken. Humus will not be replaced and nutrients in the soil will be washed away (**leached**) by the heavy rain. Within three or four years the soil becomes infertile (diagram **C**). The forest Indians overcame this problem by moving home every few years (shifting cultivation). Cattle ranchers, having cleared vast areas, now have to do the same - leaving large areas scarred and unusable. Former landless families, resettled here by the government, have seen the soil become too infertile to grow sufficient food to

A
Converting rainforest into land for cattle grazing in Brazil

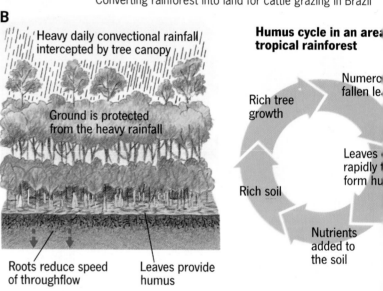

B

Heavy daily convectional rainfall intercepted by tree canopy

Ground is protected from the heavy rainfall

Roots reduce speed of throughflow

Leaves provide humus

Humus cycle in an area tropical rainforest

Numerc fallen le

Rich tree growth

Leaves rapidly form hu

Rich soil

Nutrients added to the soil

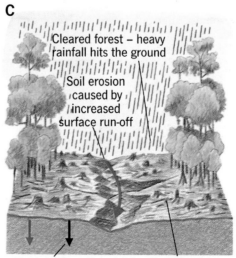

C

Cleared forest – heavy rainfall hits the ground

Soil erosion caused by increased surface run-off

Nutrients in soil washed downwards (leaching)

No fallen leaves to renew humus

The cycle after an area forest has been cleare

Fewer tr and lea

Poorer quality vegetation. Soil erosion

Les hun

Soil becomes less fertile

Few nutrients a to soil. Others a lost to plants through leachin feed themselves. Many have abandoned their new farms and moved to urban shanty settlements.

Decrease in hardwood

Only about one tree in twenty is of economic value to the timber companies, but their machinery, and falling timber, destroy many of the surrounding trees. As a result, some species, such as mahogany, greenheart and rosewood, are becoming endangered.

Carbon dioxide and oxygen balance

Deforestation means that there will no longer be trees to take in carbon dioxide and give out oxygen (page 42).

Minerals and hydro-electricity

The Brazilian rainforest includes two of the world's largest mining operations. The Carajas iron ore project (page 105) could lead to a mining and industrial complex the size of the UK and France combined (photo **D**). Bauxite, used in the production of aluminium, is mined at Trombetas. These, and other, developments will rely on the building of up to 79 massive hydro-electric power schemes by the year 2010. These schemes will, in turn, involve the flooding of large areas of land. On a smaller scale, gold is being mined by nearly a million prospectors (photo **E**). These prospectors, many of whom work illegally, destroy vegetation by using high pressure water jets and pollute water supplies with toxic mercury used in the mining process.

D Carajas iron ore mine, Amazon, Brazil

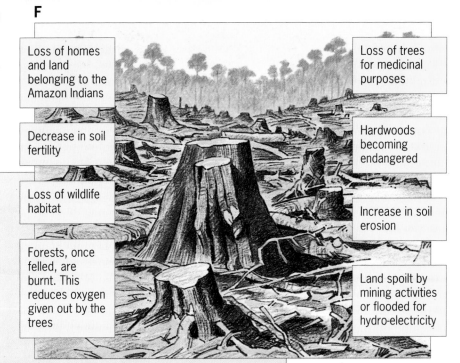

E Gold miners, Serra Pelade, Brazil

F

Loss of homes and land belonging to the Amazon Indians

Decrease in soil fertility

Loss of wildlife habitat

Forests, once felled, are burnt. This reduces oxygen given out by the trees

Loss of trees for medicinal purposes

Hardwoods becoming endangered

Increase in soil erosion

Land spoilt by mining activities or flooded for hydro-electricity

Activities

1 a) Diagram **F** suggests eight consequences of deforestation in Brazil. Describe how each affects the environment and the local community.
   b) Deforestation is taking place so that the rainforests may be economically developed. Which of the following do you consider to be the more important?
   • Economic development
   • Rainforest conservation
   Give reasons for your answer.

Summary The rainforest is, despite its apparent luxuriant vegetation, a fragile environment. There are fears that, if deforestation for economic development continues at the same rate, the rainforest will soon be totally destroyed.

41

▶ *Deforestation – is there a need for international co-operation?* ◀

Deforestation is of international concern. The rainforests are a vital natural resource which provide a wide variety of products needed by all countries. Their destruction is not only removing these resources, it is also changing world climates.

- The burning of the rainforests, and the subsequent release of carbon dioxide (a greenhouse gas), is a major cause of global warming (page 28).
- A greatly reduced number of trees will mean a decrease in evapotranspiration. With less water vapour in the air, rainfall is expected to decrease (diagram **A**). Some scientists believe this could eventually turn places like the Amazon Basin into desert.
- Trees take in carbon dioxide and, through photosynthesis, give out oxygen (diagram **A**). It is estimated that nearly one-half of the world's supply of oxygen comes from trees in the Amazon Basin. It takes one large tree to provide enough oxygen for two people for one day, and 150 large trees to absorb the carbon dioxide produced by one small car.

A

Before deforestation

Precipitation (rain) each afternoon helps rainforest to grow

Carbon dioxide given off by people, power stations and industry

Animals and people use up oxygen

CO_2 absorbed by trees (photosynthesis)

Evapo-trans-piration

Cond-ensation

Trees give off oxygen

Large amounts of water vapour in atmosphere

After deforestation

Less rainfall so area becomes drier, possibly even a desert

More CO_2 in air – increase in greenhouse gases causing global warming and climatic change

Less water vapour means less cond-ensation

Industry and power stations give off more CO_2

More people use up more oxygen

Trees burned, rainforest destroyed

Fewer trees to produce oxygen and to absorb CO_2

Fewer trees means less transpiration and so less water vapour in air

There are two extreme conflicts of interest in the rainforest. On one hand there are those groups of people who wish to use the forest to make a quick profit. On the other, there are those who wish to protect the forest and leave it exactly as it is. Caught in the middle are the people who actually live there. To them the forest is their home. They need to preserve the forest as well as being able to use its resources if they are to find work and improve their standard of living. The solution is to manage the forest in a sustainable way, using the resources carefully. Trees are a renewable resource, but only if they are used and managed carefully. At present nobody is taking responsibility for the rainforest. The forest is no longer managed in the traditional way by small scale shifting cultivators, nor by government agencies or commercial companies. This leaves the forest open to illegal logging, mining and conversion to other land uses. Such an approach benefits nobody.

Diagram **B** suggests several proposed methods of managing the rainforest. Extract **C** and photo **D** quotes an example of an attempt to manage the rainforest in a sustainable way.

Emilio Sanchoma lives in the Amazon region of Peru where rapid deforestation is taking place. He is involved in a scheme aimed at managing the forest sustainably. A similar sustainable logging project in Mindanao in the Philippines is shown in photo **D**.

B

> Create more National Parks and Forest Reserves similar to the Korup Park in the Cameroons (Africa).

> Only give logging grants to multinational companies on the condition that they replant an equal number of trees as they fell.

> Reduce international trade in such endangered hardwoods as mahogany.

> Reduce the mass burning of trees to reduce global warming and climatic change.

C

I was born in the rainforest and have lived here all my life. Like all rainforest people, I know how to harvest the forest sustainably to feed myself, my family and my tribe. I grow crops like rice to sell and other crops and fruit to eat. I also keep poultry and other animals. We use the plants of the rainforest for medicines.

As rainforest people we are worried about our own way of life and about the future of the planet. We have been trying to find better ways of using the forest. In our area, the Palcazú Valley, the government has given us title to the land. We have set up the Yanesha Forestry Co-operative to log the forest on a sustainable basis.

We clear-cut a strip of rainforest 20-50 metres wide, the same size as would be cleared if a large tree were blown down. It is wide enough to enable sunlight to penetrate the canopy and narrow enough for the plants to reseed themselves from the surrounding forest.

The trees are felled with chainsaws and then taken out by oxen onto a main logging road where they are loaded onto the co-op truck. The oxen don't damage the soil and surrounding vegetation and are less expensive than heavy machinery. We use every stick in the forest. Logs greater than 30 cm in diameter are sawn into lumber. Smaller logs between 5 and 30 cm are used for construction in our area. Smaller trees and odd-shaped

D

scraps are made into charcoal and sold locally. We get 250 cubic metres of wood per hectare under this system, compared with a typical logger's yield of 3-5 cubic metres.

Source: Global Environment, *BBC/Longman*

Activities

1 Deforestation is an international problem. How is it affecting
   i) global temperatures,
   ii) rainfall in equatorial areas,
   iii) the balance of oxygen and carbon dioxide in the atmosphere?

2 a) What is meant by the term 'to manage the rainforests in a sustainable way'?
   b) Describe one scheme which is trying 'to manage the rainforest in a sustainable way'.
   c) Why is it difficult to get international agreements which would enable the forests 'to be managed in a sustainable way'?

3 Divide your class into four groups. Each group should represent the views of one of the following: the Brazilian government; an international logging company; a group of forest Indians; and a conservation group. Each group should take their turn to put forward their case for or against the development of the rainforest.

Summary

There is a need to balance the protection and the economic development of the rainforest. Sustainable development can only come about through international co-operation and management.

► *What causes soil erosion?* ◄

The first stage in the formation of soil is when physical and chemical weathering break down the underlying rock of a place into small particles. The second stage includes the addition of water, air (including oxygen), humus (material from decayed plants) and living organisms (bacteria, worms). There are many different types of soil. They can vary in **depth, colour, texture** and **organic content** as well as in drainage, nutrients (humus) and acidity. Yet there is one thing which all soils have in common - the long period of time needed for them to form. Estimates suggest that, in Britain, it takes about 400 years for 1 cm of soil to form, and between 3000 and 12000 years for soil to become deep enough for farming. In contrast **soil erosion** can be very rapid. Several centimetres can disappear within minutes during a severe storm, while human mismanagement can cause soil to lose its fertility within a few years. Soil is a renewable source, but like water and trees, it needs careful management.

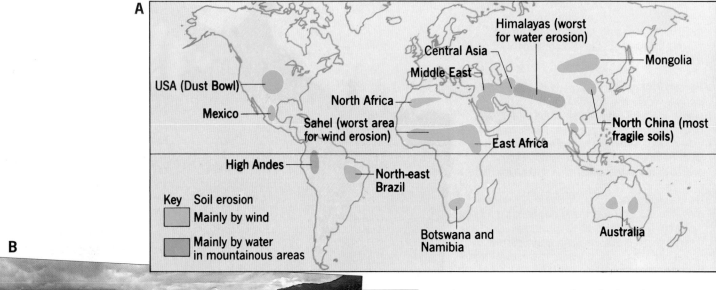

A

Himalayas (worst for water erosion)

Central Asia

Middle East

Mongolia

USA (Dust Bowl)

North Africa

Mexico

Sahel (worst area for wind erosion)

North China (most fragile soils)

East Africa

High Andes

North-east Brazil

Botswana and Namibia

Australia

Key   Soil erosion
- Mainly by wind
- Mainly by water in mountainous areas

B

Much of the land has been deforested.
The lower hillsides have been left almost bare of vegetation, and goats are busy eating what is left. It is not simply that the trees that once grew here cannot grow again, but that without its protective tree cover the soil itself is washed away. When the heavy monsoon rains come, both rain and earth are lost. Now, with the trees gone, the water runs quickly off the land, carving out new erosion channels and creating bare rock above and floods and landslides below. Great ravines are rapidly gouged out creating a man-made wilderness.

Adapted liberally from Nigel Nicolson, Himalayas, *Time-Life Books*

Soil erosion is a process by which soil is removed by the wind and running water. Soil erosion is not a major problem in places where there is permanent cover of grass or forest. It does become a problem when human activity removes this protective vegetation cover either to plough the land or through deforestation. If soil is left exposed to the weather it can be washed away during times of heavy rainfall or blown away when it dries out during times of drought. Map **A** shows those places most vulnerable to soil erosion.

- Where the land is mountainous with very steep slopes. One quarter of a million tonnes of topsoil are washed off the deforested mountain slopes of Nepal and northern India each year (extract **B**) only to be deposited into the Bay of Bengal.
- Where the climate includes a pronounced dry season and where annual rainfall totals are unreliable (page 26). When adverse human activity takes places in areas of unreliable rainfall, such as the Sahel countries in Africa, the resultant loss of soil and vegetation is known as **desertification** (page 48).

Diagram **C** shows the main causes of soil erosion. Most result from deforestation, overgrazing and overcultivation.

C

Steep slopes
eg. mountainous areas in various parts of the world

Areas with unreliable rainfall
eg. tropical continental/savanna grasslands

Tourism
Walkers enlarge footpaths. New runs for skiers.

Deforestation
a) Increases surface run-off and throughflow
b) Decreases interception and evapotranspiration

Silt (soil) blocks river. Increases flood risk and erosion of banks.

Overgrazing – Rearing too many animals in relation to amount of grass available

Heavy machinery compacts ground, reducing infiltration

Burning grass
a) By man, to force new growth for grazing
b) By lightning strikes

Autumn ploughing leaves soil unprotected during winter storms

Removing hedges or shelter belts to meet demand for fuelwood

Overcropping and monoculture (Growing crops intensively, or a single crop year after year) – crop needed for export (cash) or to feed a growing population. Lack of manure – used as fuel instead of as fertiliser.

Ploughing up and down hill creates channels down which rainwater can flow. Increases amount and speed of surface run-off.

- Washed downhill by water
- Moves slowly downwards under gravity

EXPOSED SOIL

- Washed away during wet season storms
- Blown away during dry season

Activities

1 a) How does soil form?
   b) How long does it take for soil to form?

2 a) Name two mountainous parts of the world where soil erosion is a serious problem.
   b) Give three possible causes of soil erosion in mountainous areas.

   c) Name two parts of the world with unreliable rainfall.
   d) How can unreliable and seasonal rainfall be a cause of serious soil erosion?
   e) Give three possible causes of soil erosion in places with an unreliable rainfall.

Summary

It can take several centuries for soil to form but only a short time for it to be destroyed. Soil erosion, which is greatly accelerated by human activity, is most serious on steep-sided mountainous and in places where the rainfall is unreliable.

45

▶ *What can be done to prevent or reduce soil erosion?* ◀

As the world's population continues to increase then presumably farmers are going to have to produce more food in order to feed the extra numbers. This can only be done if the soil is protected and carefully managed. Estimates suggest that by the year 2000, 20 per cent of land that was arable in 1985 will have been lost through erosion, desertification and conversion to non-agricultural uses.

By 2020 the same amount again could disappear. Although the loss is greatest in tropical economically less developed countries, it is by no means limited to those places. It is important that greater attempts are made internationally, similar to those described in case studies **A** to **D**, to reduce erosion and sustain productivity.

A

Terracing in Indonesia and the Philippines Large areas of these two countries are covered in volcanic mountains which have steep slopes and fertile soil. Over 2000 years ago terraces, which resemble giant steps, were first built on many of the hillsides. Each terrace is flat and is fronted by a mud or stone wall known as a 'bund'. The bund traps both rainwater and soil. By allowing rainwater time to infiltrate into the ground, surface run-off and the removal of topsoil is prevented.

B

C

Contour ploughing and strip cropping in the USA
Contour farming is ploughing around hillsides rather than up and down the slope. By ploughing parallel to the contours, the furrows will trap rainwater and prevent the water from washing soil downhill. Strip cropping is when two or more crops are planted in the same field. Sometimes one crop may grow under the shelter of a taller crop. It will be harvested at a different time of year and use different nutrients from the soil. Often the crops are rotated from year to year.

Animal welfare in Kenya Large herds of cattle, goats, sheep and camels have long been considered a source of wealth and prestige in several African countries. Unfortunately quantity, rather than quality, has tended to result in overgrazing. The problem of overgrazing has increased partly due to rainfall becoming even less reliable and the rapidly growing population. Intermediate Technology, a British organisation, is working with local people in several parts of Kenya. In those areas it is helping to train one person from each a village to become a 'wasaidizi' or animal care worker. By recognising and being able to treat basic animal illnesses, the wasaidizi is improving the quality of local herds. As the quality improves there should be less need for as many animals so that, hopefully, overgrazing will be reduced.

D

Stone lines ('magic stones') in Burkina Faso

This project, begun by Oxfam in 1979, uses appropriate technology, local knowledge and local raw materials. It involves villagers, of all ages and both sexes, collecting some of the many stones lying around their village. The stones are laid across the land to stop surface run-off following the all too rare heavy rainstorms. Water and soil are trapped. The water then has time to infiltrate instead of being lost immediately through surface run-off. The soil soon becomes deep enough for the planting of crops. Erosion is reduced and crop yields have increased by as much as 50 per cent. The only equipment needed is a simple level, developed by Oxfam, to help keep the lines parallel to the contours.

Activities

1 Diagram **E** shows several methods aimed at reducing soil erosion.
   a) Briefly describe each method.
   b) Which methods are appropriate to Britain?

E

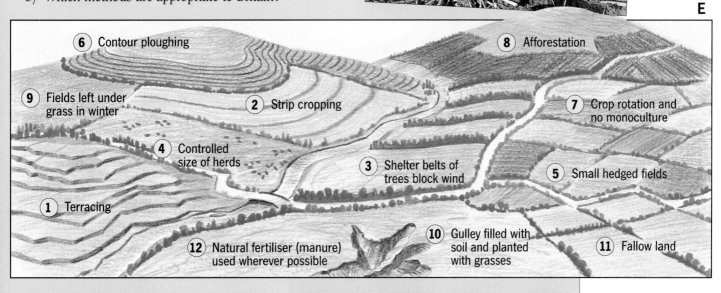

- (6) Contour ploughing
- (8) Afforestation
- (9) Fields left under grass in winter
- (2) Strip cropping
- (7) Crop rotation and no monoculture
- (4) Controlled size of herds
- (3) Shelter belts of trees block wind
- (5) Small hedged fields
- (1) Terracing
- (10) Gulley filled with soil and planted with grasses
- (11) Fallow land
- (12) Natural fertiliser (manure) used wherever possible

2 Photo **F** shows a soil conservation poster used in Kenya. It was designed in cartoon form by a local artist who used local examples of afforestation, terracing and controlled grazing.
   a) What are the advantages of providing educational information in this way?
   b) Which methods of soil conservation are likely to be of most value to an economically developing country with unreliable rainfall and a growing population such as Kenya?
   c) Why is it often difficult for an economically developing country to introduce these methods?

F

Summary

Soil is a renewable resource but only if it is managed carefully. All countries must make greater efforts if soil erosion is to be prevented and reduced so that soil productivity can be sustained.

▶ *What causes desertification?* ◀

'Turning land into desert' is the simplest of several definitions of desertification. Desertification occurs mainly in semi-arid lands which border the world's major deserts. Map **A** is often misinterpreted. It locates places which are at risk from desertification, **not** places where desertification has actually occurred. The area at greatest risk is the Sahel, a narrow belt of land extending across Africa and lying to the south of the Sahara Desert.

A

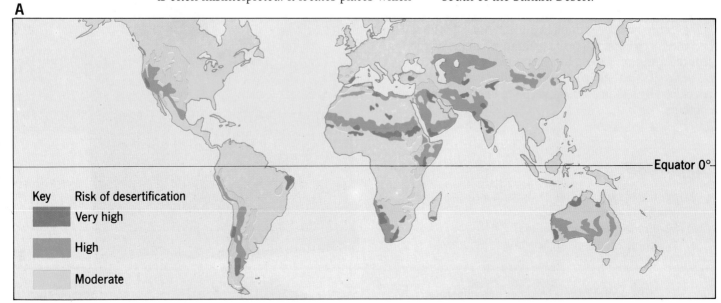

Key   Risk of desertification

Very high

High

Moderate

Equator 0°

The causes of desertification are complex. They appear to result from a combination of climatic changes (e.g. decreased rainfall and global warming) with increased human activity and pressure upon the land (e.g. overgrazing, overcultivation and deforestation). How these factors may have contributed to desertification is shown on diagram **B**. During the 1980s it was claimed, and accepted, that the Sahara was advancing southwards at a rate of between 6 and 10 km a year. However, many claims were little more than estimates based upon short-term observations, and they were made at the height of one of Africa's worst ever recorded droughts. The drought, which began in the early 1970s, followed two wet decades (graph **C**).

B

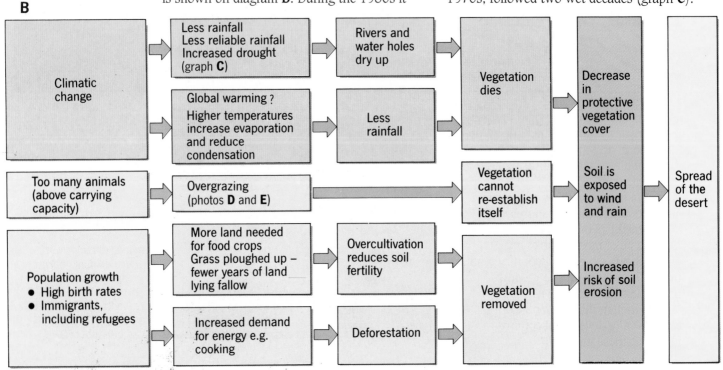

Climatic change	Less rainfall / Less reliable rainfall / Increased drought (graph **C**)	Rivers and water holes dry up	Vegetation dies	Decrease in protective vegetation cover	Spread of the desert
	Global warming? / Higher temperatures increase evaporation and reduce condensation	Less rainfall			
Too many animals (above carrying capacity)	Overgrazing (photos **D** and **E**)		Vegetation cannot re-establish itself	Soil is exposed to wind and rain	
Population growth • High birth rates • Immigrants, including refugees	More land needed for food crops / Grass ploughed up – fewer years of land lying fallow	Overcultivation reduces soil fertility	Vegetation removed	Increased risk of soil erosion	
	Increased demand for energy e.g. cooking	Deforestation			

During that wetter period farmers began to grow crops on land which had not been cultivated for several centuries, and to crowd larger herds of livestock onto smaller areas of pasture. When this was replaced by a much drier period it looked as if the land was being overcultivated and overgrazed. Within a few years over 100 000 people and millions of animals died. The initial investigations for those deaths and, later, for many more in Ethiopia, the Sudan and Somalia, put the blame on desertification.

C

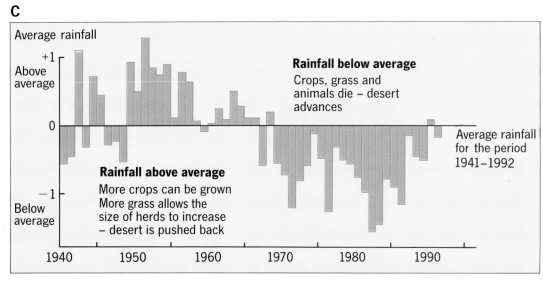

Average rainfall

Rainfall below average
Crops, grass and animals die – desert advances

Rainfall above average
More crops can be grown
More grass allows the size of herds to increase – desert is pushed back

Average rainfall for the period 1941–1992

Recently the claim that the Sahara is advancing has been disputed. Evidence, based mainly on satellite images, does show annual changes resulting from variations in rainfall, but no permanent advance. This does not, of course, mean that the risk has disappeared. Hopefully, the threat of desertification has increased people's awareness of the semi-arid lands as a fragile environment. Their boundaries are constantly changing as a result of variations in rainfall, and it is difficult to separate natural causes from human activity (e.g. Is overgrazing a result of increased drought or increased human activity - photos **D** and **E**?). Regardless of whether desertification is already a major hazard or whether it is a future risk, one thing is certain: increased desertification is likely, as with all environmental issues, to result from people's misuse of natural resources.

D Goats, sheep and camels drinking at a well, Sudan

E
Overgrazed area,
Burkina Faso

Activities

1 a) What is desertification?
 b) Name, with the help of an atlas, six Sahel countries.
 c) Desertification is blamed upon physical processes and human activity. Explain how the following might have combined to cause desertification:
   i) changes in rainfall and global warming.
   ii) overgrazing, overcultivation and deforestation.

2 What recent evidence seems to contradict the claim that desertification is increasing?

Summary

Desertification in semi-arid lands may result from a combination of physical processes and human activity. Recent evidence suggests that, although the risks remain high, the increase in desertification may be less than was previously claimed.

▶ *Why are wetland environments fragile?* ◀

A

Key

▲ Wetland

● Selected Ramsar sites

■ Wildfowl and wetlands trust centres

Caer Laverock (Scotland)

N

Washington

Dee Estuary

Martin Mere

Humber Estuary

The Wash

Peakirk

Welney

Llanelli

Severn

Severn Estuary and Cardiff Bay

Slimbridge

Thames Estuary

Solent

Swale

Arundel

Chesil Beach

Chichester and Langstone harbours

0   100 km

Wetlands form a transition environment between land and water. As the water table is usually near to, or even at, the surface then the land is either permanently or seasonally covered with water. The water may be either slow-flowing, stagnant, brackish, fresh or salt. This produces several different types of wetland including coastal estuaries, river floodplains, freshwater marshes, peatlands and mangrove swamps. Most of Britain's largest remaining wetlands are in river estuaries (map **A**). Estuaries are places where salt and fresh water mix and where tidal action is important. As a result estuaries have developed a special ecosystem of their own (diagram **B**).

B

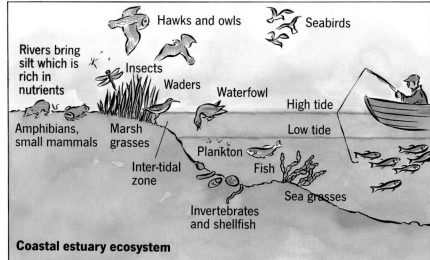

Hawks and owls   Seabirds

Rivers bring silt which is rich in nutrients

Insects

Waders

Waterfowl

High tide

Low tide

Amphibians, small mammals

Marsh grasses

Plankton

Fish

Inter-tidal zone

Invertebrates and shellfish

Sea grasses

Coastal estuary ecosystem

Why are coastal wetlands important?

Wetlands are among the world's most productive ecosystems (photos **C**, **D** and **F**). They:

- are often very fertile and can produce eight times more plant matter than the average field of wheat.
- provide a life support system for a wide range of plants, birds, fish and insects.
- provide a nursery for young fish and a winter feeding ground for birds.
- help to filter pollution and sediment out of water.
- slow down the speed of water and, since they can store excess water following storms, they help to reduce the danger of flooding.
- can provide jobs, especially in aquaculture (fish farming) and on nature reserves.

C Everglades National Park, Florida

D Mersey Estuary, Widnes

Why are many coastal wetlands under threat?

- Parts of wetlands have always been used for pasture farming and, if sufficiently well drained, can provide rich soil for crops.
- If water is extracted for domestic and industrial purposes then the water table will fall causing the land to sink. Floodbanks are needed where the land sinks below river or sea levels.
- A falling water table can result in reeds and other plants dying and wild life habitats being lost.
- There is an increasing number of tourists and tourist-related activities. Tourists disturb wildlife and their boats produce waves which erode banks and destroy nesting grounds.
- Increased pollution from diesel oil from pleasure boats or, from further upstream, run-off from farmland and waste from industry.

The greatest threat to all coastal wetlands is likely to come from the predicted rise in the world's sea-level resulting from global warming (page 29).

How can wetlands be protected?

Over 60 countries have now signed an international agreement called the Ramsar Convention. This Convention, first signed by several countries in 1971, is the oldest global conservation treaty (diagram **G**). International agreement is necessary as many wetlands extend across national boundaries. Since 1971 there has been a changed emphasis on protection and use of wetlands (extract **E**).

E

Now, the value of a wetland as an example of a type characteristic of its region, or its value to a wide range of animals and plants, or even its socio-economic value to local communities, are all considered important. Parties must promote the conservation of sites, but this does not mean strict 'hands-off' protection. Provided the natural characteristics of the ecosystem are maintained, Parties are encouraged to use Ramsar sites on a sustainable basis, and many more sites are exploited for the benefit of local people.

Worldwide Fund for Nature (WWF)

The Camargue wetland is in the Rhône Delta in France. It is home to herds of white horses, thousands of flamingoes and wintering, breeding and migrating wild birds. The wetland is threatened by housing developments, tourism, farming, drainage and industrial development.

F

G

Plan a sustainable use for wetlands

Encourage research into wetland ecosystems

Train people in wetland management

Develop a national policy on wetland conservation

Create nature and wildfowl reserves

Work with neighbouring countries on schemes which cross national borders

Activities

1 a) What are wetlands?
   b) Why is it considered important to protect wetlands and their ecosystems?
   c) How, according to diagram **G**, has the Ramsar Convention attempted to protect wetlands?

2 a) Make a copy of table **H** and complete it using information from these pages.
   b) If you had to develop a new wildfowl reserve what
      i) facilities would you provide to attract visitors;
      ii) precautions would you take to ensure that the visitors did not harm the wildlife habitat?

H

Threat to wetland ecosystem	Possible effects on wildlife and ecosystem

Summary

Wetlands are a fragile environment lying between land and water. They have developed a productive, but now a greatly threatened, ecosystem.

6 The European Union (EU)

▶ What are the patterns of tourism in the EU? ◀

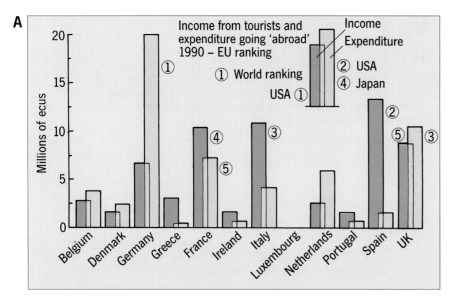

A

Income from tourists and expenditure going 'abroad' 1990 – EU ranking

- Income
- Expenditure
- ① World ranking

② USA
④ Japan

Countries (x-axis): Belgium, Denmark, Germany, Greece, France, Ireland, Italy, Luxembourg, Netherlands, Portugal, Spain, UK

Y-axis: Millions of ecus (0 to 20)

Rankings shown: Germany ①, Greece, France ④ ⑤, Italy ③, Netherlands ①② ④ (USA ①, USA ②, Japan ④), Spain ②, UK ⑤ ③

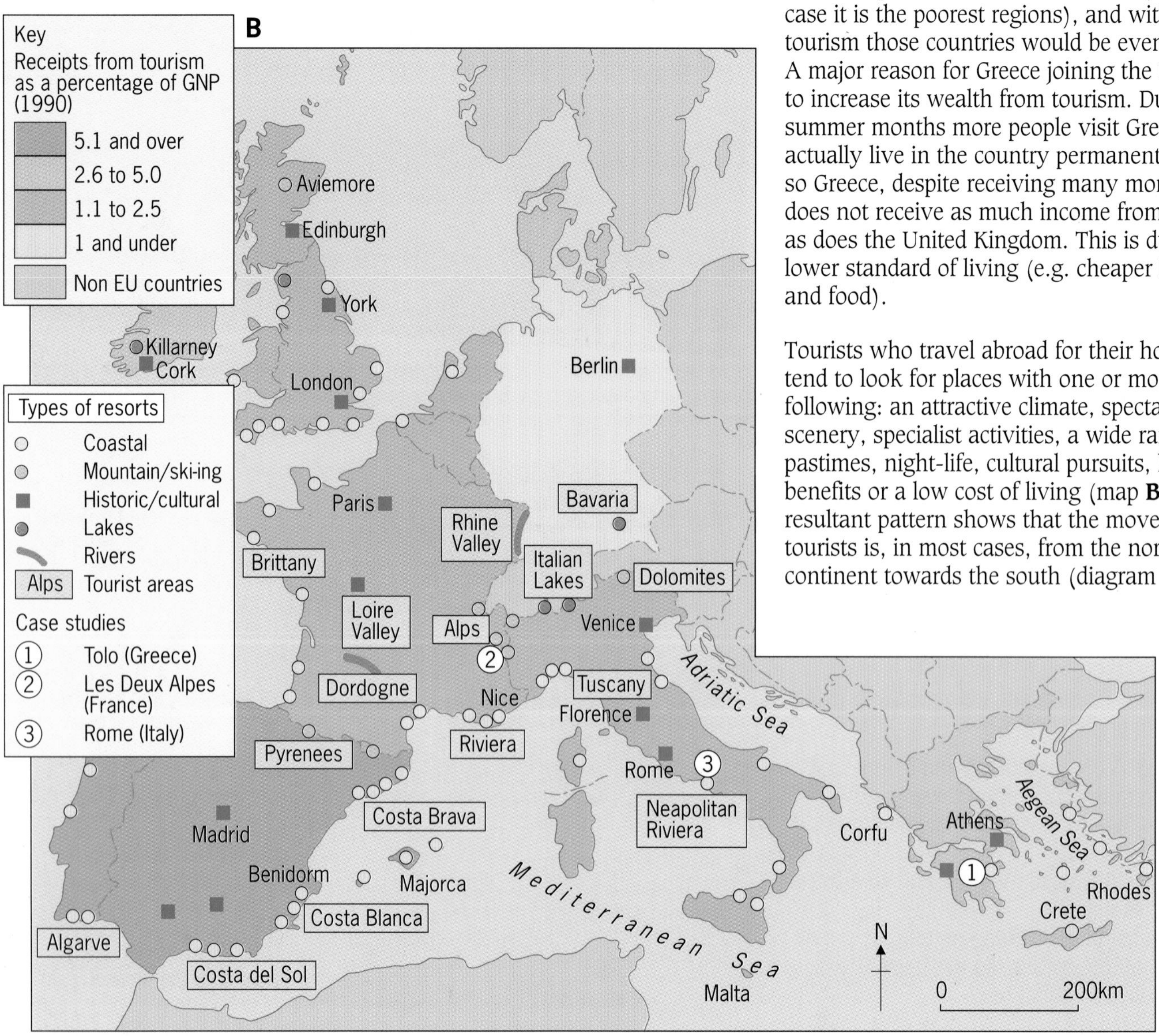

Article 2 of the Treaty of Rome (1957) gives the European Community (EC), now the European Union (EU), power to 'promote closer relations between the states which belong to it'. One way to achieve this is through tourism. Tourism, a labour-intensive industry, was believed to have provided 4 million jobs in 1980, and 8.5 million in 1990. If it reaches the predicted total of 12 million by the turn of the century, it will be the largest single employer in the EU. Yet, strangely, EU ministers do not appear to see tourism as a high priority.

Graph **A** shows how important tourism is to many countries within the EU. The 'southern' countries earn more from tourism than their residents spend abroad. The net 'gainers' tend to be the poorer countries in the EU (in Italy's case it is the poorest regions), and without tourism those countries would be even poorer. A major reason for Greece joining the EU was to increase its wealth from tourism. During the summer months more people visit Greece than actually live in the country permanently. Even so Greece, despite receiving many more visitors, does not receive as much income from tourism as does the United Kingdom. This is due to its lower standard of living (e.g. cheaper hotels and food).

Tourists who travel abroad for their holidays tend to look for places with one or more of the following: an attractive climate, spectacular scenery, specialist activities, a wide range of pastimes, night-life, cultural pursuits, health benefits or a low cost of living (map **B**). The resultant pattern shows that the movement of tourists is, in most cases, from the north of the continent towards the south (diagram **C**).

B

Key

Receipts from tourism as a percentage of GNP (1990)

- 5.1 and over
- 2.6 to 5.0
- 1.1 to 2.5
- 1 and under
- Non EU countries

Types of resorts

- ○ Coastal
- ◒ Mountain/ski-ing
- ■ Historic/cultural
- ◓ Lakes
- ～ Rivers
- Alps Tourist areas

Case studies

- ① Tolo (Greece)
- ② Les Deux Alpes (France)
- ③ Rome (Italy)

Map labels: Aviemore, Edinburgh, York, Killarney, Cork, London, Berlin, Paris, Bavaria, Rhine Valley, Italian Lakes, Dolomites, Brittany, Loire Valley, Alps ②, Venice, Tuscany, Dordogne, Nice, Florence, Adriatic Sea, Riviera, Rome ③, Pyrenees, Neapolitan Riviera, Corfu, Athens ①, Costa Brava, Madrid, Benidorm, Majorca, Costa Blanca, Algarve, Costa del Sol, Mediterranean Sea, Malta, Aegean Sea, Rhodes, Crete

N

0   200km

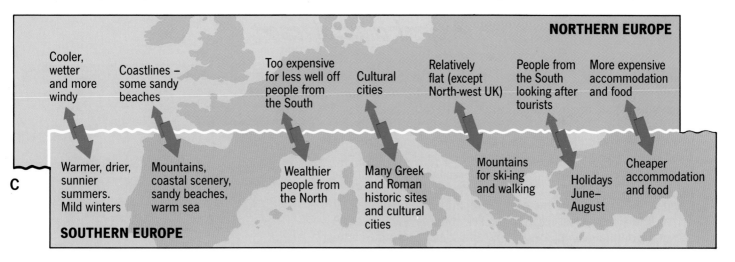

NORTHERN EUROPE

Cooler, wetter and more windy

Coastlines – some sandy beaches

Too expensive for less well off people from the South

Cultural cities

Relatively flat (except North-west UK)

People from the South looking after tourists

More expensive accommodation and food

C

Warmer, drier, sunnier summers. Mild winters

Mountains, coastal scenery, sandy beaches, warm sea

Wealthier people from the North

Many Greek and Roman historic sites and cultural cities

Mountains for ski-ing and walking

Holidays June–August

Cheaper accommodation and food

SOUTHERN EUROPE

EU tourism policies include:
- providing money from the European Regional Development Fund. This is used to encourage tourism in areas which have potential but have a low standard of living and a high unemployment rate, e.g. Mezzogiorno (southern Italy).
- encouraging craft industries and specialist activities to try to reduce regional and rural depopulation (page 79).
- integrating cross-continental transport routes (the 'E' road and 'Eurail' networks).
- improving access to newly developing resorts and holiday areas (e.g. southern Greece).
- protecting the natural environment (beaches, seas and wildlife) and the cultural environment (ancient sites and historic buildings).
- improving tourist services and amenities, such as water and electricity supplies, sewerage; improving safety in hotels; providing regulation camping and caravan sites.
- removing, or in some cases reducing, border controls and customs checks (diagram **D**).

Border controls between some EU countries vanished in 1993. Passport checks became lighter throughout the EU.

There is a new blue channel at customs and millions of pages of customs forms have disappeared. Consumers can buy alcohol, tobacco and other products for personal use without limits.

D

A totally border-free Europe did not exist on 1 January 1993. Britain, Denmark, Greece and Ireland have retained some checks and controls.

New rules mean some qualifications are now recognised throughout the EU, making it easier for people to work abroad

Activities

1. a) Name five EU countries which receive more money from foreign tourists than their own inhabitants spend in other countries.
   b) Describe the location within the EU of these five countries.
   c) Name five EU countries whose inhabitants spend more in foreign countries than they receive from tourists from other countries.
   d) Describe the location within the EU of these five countries.

2. a) Copy and complete table **E** by naming three countries which best fit each description.
   b) Draw a star diagram to describe five ways in which EU policy has affected tourism. Use these headings to help you:
      · jobs, transport, environment, services, accommodation.

E

	Country or region		
	1	2	3
Hot, dry, sunny summers; mild winters			
Sandy beaches, warm seas			
Ski-ing in winter; mountain climbing in summer			
Castles, cathedrals, ancient sites			
Earn most from tourism			
Cooler, wetter, less sunny			
More industry and so less attractive			
Fewer mountains; less opportunities for ski-ing			
Spend more on tourism than is earned			

Summary

Tourism is one of the EU's most important sources of employment and income. It is most important to some of the poorer but warmer, drier and sunnier parts of southern Europe. EU policies have had a limited impact upon the continued development of tourism.

► *A Greek coastal resort* ◄

Tolo is located in the Peloponnese peninsula and to the south-west of Athens (map **A**). It has a long, sandy, sheltered and curving beach which stretches over 3 km between two rocky headlands.

In 1979 Tolo was still an unspoilt village with a linear shape. Many small shops selling local produce extended either side of the one long and narrow main street. The major occupations were farming (mainly fruit) and fishing. The only tourists were Athenians escaping in summer from the heat, noise and pollution of their city. Today Tolo is the largest resort in the Peloponnese. Landsketch **B** shows the natural advantages of Tolo and some of its added tourist amenities. It also gives some of the causes of pollution and conflict in the present resort. Tourism brings both benefits and problems.

A

GREECE

Delphi △

Corinth Canal ■ Athens

Olympia △   Mycenae △   △ Epidauros

Tolo ■

Peloponnese

Key

△ Classical site

☐ Highland

0   100 km

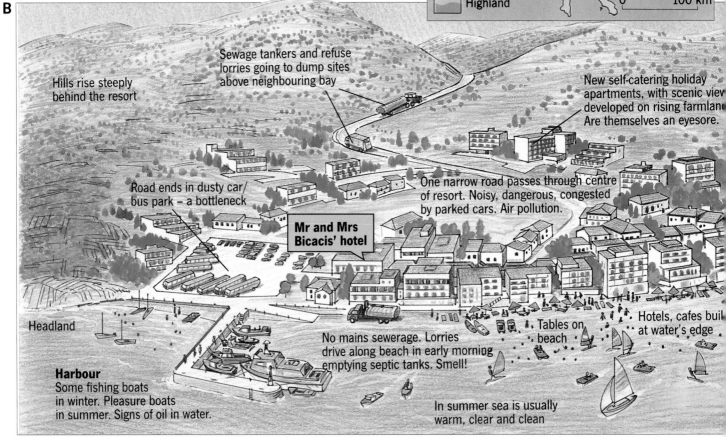

B

Sewage tankers and refuse lorries going to dump sites above neighbouring bay

Hills rise steeply behind the resort

New self-catering holiday apartments, with scenic view developed on rising farmland Are themselves an eyesore.

Road ends in dusty car/ bus park – a bottleneck

One narrow road passes through centre of resort. Noisy, dangerous, congested by parked cars. Air pollution.

Mr and Mrs Bicacis' hotel

Headland

Tables on beach

Hotels, cafes built at water's edge

No mains sewerage. Lorries drive along beach in early morning emptying septic tanks. Smell!

Harbour
Some fishing boats in winter. Pleasure boats in summer. Signs of oil in water.

In summer sea is usually warm, clear and clean

C   Tolo – the natural setting

D   Tolo – added amenities

E

Nikos and Katarina Bicacis

Mr and Mrs Bicacis live behind the hotel which they run together. As the holiday season is so short, Mr Bicacis also runs a farm 20 km away. Their working year is:

◆ **March** Hotel opens; very quiet.

◆ **May to August** The hotel is very busy and extra domestic help is needed. While tourists like the hot, dry weather, it does not help the farm where crops (mainly fruit) need to be watered each day.

◆ **September** Hotel is quiet.

◆ **October/November** Domestic staff are laid off. Repairs and redecorating jobs are done in the hotel.

◆ **December to February** Hotel is closed. This is the busiest time on the farm for oranges, the major crop.

Hot, dry sunny summers. Increased risk of water shortage for new hotels and apartments, and for farming. Winter rainfall is not sufficient to replace the water taken from ground in summer. Farmers get water from boreholes which are becoming salty.

Only one narrow road into resort. Busy in summer, noisy, little room to pass

New apartments built on farmland

Hotels, cafes, tavernas and craft shops all close for several months in winter

Former local shops turned into craft and souvenir shops. Tavernas and bars are noisy at night.

Remains of a Mycenaean settlement 3500 years old

Sand dunes

Thin sandy beach, now only 3 m wide as new hotels are built at the tideless water's edge

Sea and sand dunes polluted with litter from tourists

Sea full of swimmers, pedalos, windsurfers and yachts, all competing for the same space

Headland

Activities

1 a) Describe the appearance of Tolo in 1970.
   b) What natural advantages did Tolo possess to attract tourists?
   c) What amenities had been added by 1990 to attract more tourists to the resort?

2 Tourism can brings advantages and can create problems and conflicts. Use the

information on these two pages to answer these questions.
   a) What advantages has tourism brought to Tolo?
   b) What problems has tourism created?
   c) What conflicts have been created between
      • groups of local people;
      • local people and tourists;
      • groups of tourists?

Summary

People are attracted to Mediterranean resorts because of the hot, dry summer weather, the spectacular scenery and the added tourist amenities. Local residents, often poor by EU standards, see tourism as an opportunity to improve their standard of living even if it also changes their way of life and spoils their environment.

A French mountain resort

Les Deux Alpes is a purpose-built ski resort in the French Alps (photo **A**). It was originally two separate summer pasture areas which have been joined together by a long main road. The village is perched 1650 metres above sea-level on a sunny, rocky shelf. The only access from the valley below is by a narrow, steep road where the hairpin bends make driving difficult but provide a challenging stage for the annual 'Tour de France' cycle race. Behind the village, the Alps rise to almost 4000 metres, and there is access to both glacier and high altitude ski-ing. Snow continues to lie, at higher altitudes, throughout the summer. This enables the village to attract walkers, climbers and those people who just wish to breathe the fresh mountain air or to admire the spectacular scenery.

As in any ski resort, numerous amenities have been added (landsketch **B**). Apart from a funicular railway, which goes under the Mont de Lans glacier to reach the highest runs,

there are three cable-cars, two gondolas, 15 chair and 44 drag lifts. There are over 160 km of piste which include the widest possible range of difficulty. The resort itself consists of the main street which is lined with cafés, bars, discos and restaurants. Several hotels are located in the centre to be as near as possible to the ski-lifts and other amenities. Chalets offer cheaper accommodation and are sited on the edges of the village, further away from the main amenities. Les Deux Alpes has three sports and fitness centres, a swimming pool, a skating rink complex and a cinema.

A Les Deux Alpes

B

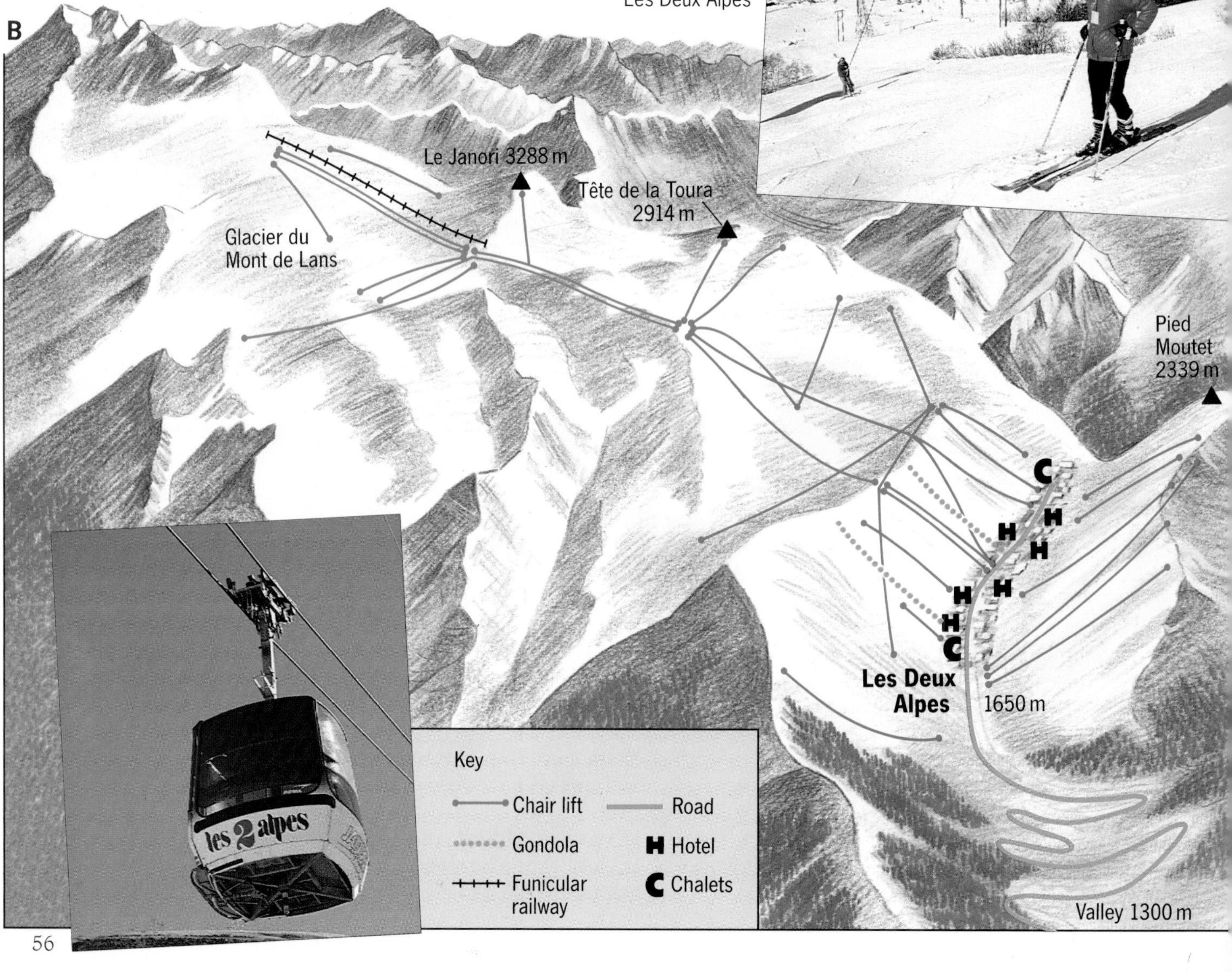

Le Janori 3288 m

Tête de la Toura 2914 m

Glacier du Mont de Lans

Pied Moutet 2339 m

Les Deux Alpes 1650 m

Key

- Chair lift
- Gondola
- Funicular railway
- Road
- **H** Hotel
- **C** Chalets

Valley 1300 m

56

The French government has encouraged the development of ski resorts and the improvement of facilities in the Alps. Although ski-ing has become increasingly popular and affordable to a greater number of people since the 1960s, it was the early 1980s which proved to be the boom years for winter sports. Unemployment fell by three per cent in ski areas whereas in the rest of France it rose by three per cent. Younger people no longer had to leave the area to look for work. Tourists spent money not only in hotels and souvenir shops, but also on skis and ski clothing. Since the mid-1980s the number of tourists has decreased. This has partly been due to several mild winters during which there was a shortage of snow, and partly due to the economic recession in Europe. Resorts have also been affected by cheaper ski holidays in other countries and increased competition from new purpose-built ski centres within France.

National governments hope to increase employment and property developers want large and quick profits. They have not always considered the effects that purpose-built ski resorts may have upon the environment or the traditional way of life of local communities. Some of the resultant problems have been summarised in table **C**.

C

Environmental impact
Deforestation of slopes for new and longer ski runs, and for new and expanding resorts
Loss of vegetation caused by ski-ing on thin snow
Visual pollution from ski-lifts and resorts built on hillsides
Less snow lower down makes skiers 'climb' higher onto fragile environments at higher altitudes
Acid rain killing vegetation in Alpine areas has been blamed on huge increase in traffic

Social impact
Seasonal unemployment as most jobs are limited to the winter ski-ing season
Farmers and forestry workers have lost jobs as ski-ing takes over the area
Traditional way of life has changed due to increase in traffic and people
House prices rise and become too expensive for local people

D

Activities

1 a) What were the natural (physical) advantages of Les Deux Alpes as a ski resort? List your points under the two headings of 'Climate' and 'Relief'.
   b) What purpose-built amenities have been added to attract tourists to Les Deux Alpes?

2 Draw a simple sketch of photo **D**. On it label the following.
   a) Three physical advantages. (Think about climate, scenery and relief.)
   b) Three purpose-built amenities. (Think of accommodation, access and ski facilities.)
   c) Three ways in which the local environment has, or may be, spoilt.

3 How can the building of a purpose-built ski resort
   a) be an advantage to local people?
   b) create problems for local people and their environment?

Summary   Mountainous areas in Europe have become increasingly popular for winter sports. Both national and local governments have encouraged the growth of new ski resorts and improved facilities. The impact of purpose-built resorts upon local communities and the environment has not always been considered.

An Italian cultural centre

A

The term **cultural**, taken in its widest sense, means learning about another country's civilisation and customs at a particular time in its history, e.g. ancient Greece, Rome and Egypt. In this sense the term covers the development of religions and so includes places of religious pilgrimage such as Rome and Makkah (Mecca). The term can also be applied, in a more narrow sense, to mean the creative activity and imagination of a group of people. This creativity includes traditional arts such as painting, architecture, sculpture and music, as well as present-day fashions in, for example, clothes and food.

Television programmes, in particular, have made a greater number of people aware of other countries' lifestyles, both past and present. An increasing number of people in the economically more developed countries have become more wealthy and have longer and paid holidays, and transport has become faster and cheaper. As a result greater numbers of people have turned to 'cultural

visits', and some combine these visits with the more traditional 'beach holiday' (e.g. visits to Thailand or Turkey).

Rome is one of many cultural centres in the EU. Tourists visit the city for many reasons.

Historical
Rome was the centre of the Roman Empire. Excavations have uncovered the remains of many buildings which date back to that time. At the centre of Roman life was the Forum with its temples, triumphal arches, monuments and, later, Christian churches. Nearby is, perhaps, the most famous of Rome's ancient buildings - the Colosseum (photo **B**).

Religious
Within Rome is the independent state of the Vatican. The Vatican, dominated by the Cathedral church of St Peter's (photo **C**), is the residence of the Pope. Each year, and especially at the times of the major Christian festivals of Christmas and Easter, many Catholics make a pilgrimage to Rome hoping to receive the Pope's blessing.

B The Colosseum

C Cathedral church of St Peter's

Culture

Italy has, arguably, produced more famous artists than any other country. The Vatican Museum, one of many museums and art galleries within Rome, is visited by most tourists. Probably the most famous part of the museum is the Sistine Chapel with its magnificent ceiling painted by Michelangelo. The nine panels (one is shown in photo **D**) took four years to paint.

Rome is full of statues and monuments dating from Roman times up to the present day. One popular tourist attraction is the Trevi Fountain (photo **E**). It is said that if you throw a coin into the fountain you are sure to revisit Rome. Rome is also noted for its architecture, especially its majestically designed piazzas (squares) and streets. More recently the city has become one of the world's leading fashion centres, and is renowned for its food and drink.

Large numbers of tourists are good for local economies. Yet while they bring in money and create jobs, the extra pressure that they put upon sites also creates many problems. There are often lengthy queues of people waiting to get into the Sistine Chapel, and flash photography is not allowed there or in art galleries because the bright light destroys the colours of the paintings. Some buildings in the Forum and parts of the Colosseum have had to be roped off to stop people climbing over them. The many tourist buses and cars cause parking problems and add to traffic congestion. They also cause vibrations, which affect the foundations of buildings, and release chemicals which erode buildings and statues. Some sites are ruined visually by souvenir and refreshment stalls, and the litter left by tourists. Tourists, especially when wealthy, can also increase the cost of living for local people.

D Part of the ceiling of the Sistine Chapel

E The Trevi Fountain

Activities

1 a) If you decided to go on a cultural holiday, what sort of things would you expect to do and to see?
   b) Why is Rome a popular centre for a cultural holiday?
   c) Name a place (town or country) which you might like to visit for a short cultural holiday. Give reasons for your choice.

2 Draw a star diagram to describe some of the problems which might occur at Rome's most popular tourist sites.

Summary

Cultural holidays have become more fashionable as beach holidays have become less popular. Many people enjoy visiting places where the life-style is very different to their own. This increase in tourism has advantages but it also creates problems.

▶ What are the patterns of migration in the EU? ◀

Geographers look for patterns. In the case of migration they look to see if there are patterns of movement between places, or patterns of movement over a period of time. Map **A** shows recent migrations between countries in Europe and graph **B** shows when those movements took place. The most obvious patterns are described below.

- Between 1945 and 1973 the countries of western Europe had more job vacancies than they had workers. Britain and France encouraged people to move from their former colonies in the West Indies and North Africa. West Germany accepted large numbers of migrants from the poorer parts of South-east Europe and Turkey. For the migrants there was the main attraction of finding better-paid jobs, together with greater opportunities to improve their standards of housing and education.
- Around 1973 several western European countries introduced new laws which tried to control the number of

immigrants. Between 1973 and the late 1980s the need for extra workers in western Europe decreased. Migration was discouraged during times of economic recession (the early 1980s) when jobs were in short supply. During this time immigrants were often restricted to members of families already living and working in the receiving country.

- Since the late 1980s there has been a huge movement of voluntary migrants, mainly ethnic Germans, from eastern Europe and what used to be the USSR. This movement peaked in late 1989 after the Berlin Wall was pulled down. The number of migrants has been considerably increased by asylum-seekers (refugees) forced by civil war to leave their homes in the former Yugoslavia. Graph **B** shows that over 70 per cent of this latest wave of migrants have tried to settle in the recently re-unified Germany.

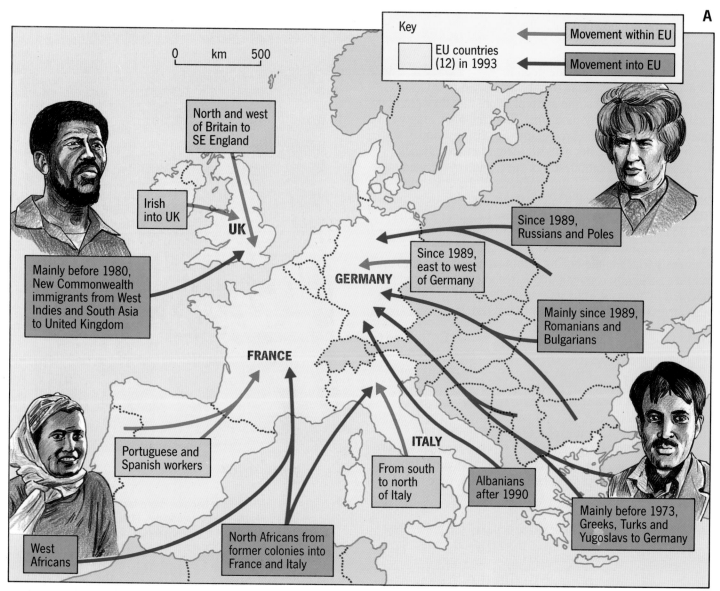

A

Key

EU countries (12) in 1993

Movement within EU

Movement into EU

0 km 500

North and west of Britain to SE England

Irish into UK

UK

Since 1989, Russians and Poles

Since 1989, east to west of Germany

GERMANY

Mainly before 1980, New Commonwealth immigrants from West Indies and South Asia to United Kingdom

Mainly since 1989, Romanians and Bulgarians

FRANCE

Portuguese and Spanish workers

ITALY

From south to north of Italy

Albanians after 1990

Mainly before 1973, Greeks, Turks and Yugoslavs to Germany

West Africans

North Africans from former colonies into France and Italy

B

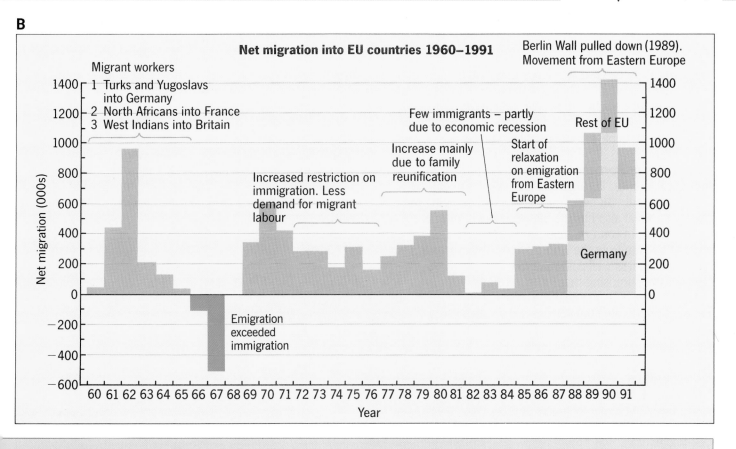

Net migration into EU countries 1960–1991

Migrant workers
1 Turks and Yugoslavs into Germany
2 North Africans into France
3 West Indians into Britain

Berlin Wall pulled down (1989). Movement from Eastern Europe

Few immigrants – partly due to economic recession

Increase mainly due to family reunification

Increased restriction on immigration. Less demand for migrant labour

Start of relaxation on emigration from Eastern Europe

Rest of EU

Germany

Emigration exceeded immigration

Net migration (000s)

Year

Activities

1 Copy out and complete the sentences below by choosing the correct answer from the choice given in brackets.

- Britain and France received many immigrants from (former colonies/South-east Europe/ Eastern Europe).
- For Britain this included (Turkey/the West Indies/North Africa) and for France (Turkey/the West Indies/North Africa).
- All these places were in (developed/developing) continents.
- Before 1973 most of West Germany's immigrants came from (the West Indies/North Africa/South-east Europe and Turkey), especially the two countries of (the former USSR/Greece/ Italy/the former Yugoslavia).
- Recently Germany has received many voluntary migrants from (Turkey/the former Yugoslavia/ Eastern Europe) and forced migrants from (Turkey/the former Yugoslavia/Eastern Europe).

2 The newspaper headlines opposite give causes of migration into and between EU countries. Rearrange the headlines in two columns headed
  - Migration into the EU
  - Migration between EU countries.

3 Most migrants into the EU between 1945 and 1973 came from different places to those migrants who have arrived since the late 1980s.
  a) From which places did most migrants come
    i) between 1945 and 1973?
    ii) since the late 1980s?
  b) Give reasons why each group migrated.

C

Germany, France and Britain short of skilled labour

Portugal has lowest standard of living in EU

Civil war in Yugoslavia

France and Britain take in workers from their colonies

High unemployment in Greece and Portugal

Russia allows residents to leave

Berlin Wall pulled down

Germany, France and Britain short of unskilled labour

Germany's laws allow in all refugees

Summary

Early migrants into the EU were encouraged to come to find work. Later arrivals saw the move to be a chance to join families or improve their standard of living. Many recent arrivals have come to escape political unrest and economic hardship in their home country.

▶ *Why migrate between EU countries?* ◀

Migrant Portuguese workers in France

In countries where there is a low standard of living and a shortage of jobs, groups of people will migrate to nearby, wealthier countries hoping to find work. One example is the movement of people from Portugal to France.

Conditions in Portugal Of the twelve present EU member countries, Portugal has the lowest standard of living. With only 38 per cent of its population living in towns, Portugal also has the highest proportion of people in Europe living in country areas and earning a living from the land. As rural jobs are less well paid than town jobs it is not surprising that Portuguese workers are paid the least per hour and receive the EU's lowest average annual salary. As in other farming communities families tend to be large and, often because there is little machinery, work on the farm is hard. As individual farms are small in size it means younger members of the family have to move to seek work elsewhere.

Many Portuguese have moved to France hoping to find temporary but better-paid work (map **A**).

When people migrate it can greatly affect the population structure of both the losing and the receiving country (graph **B**). It is usually people in the younger, more active age groups who move, leaving an increasingly elderly population at home. The much higher proportion of migrant males means divisions in families, especially among those with young children.

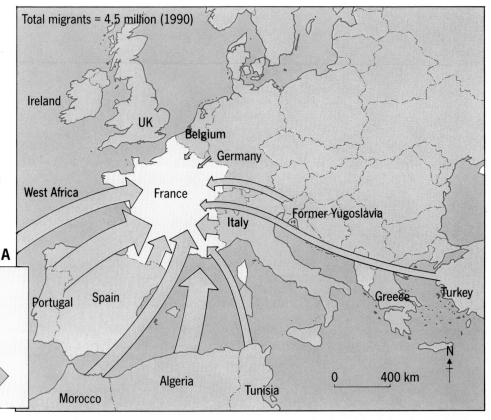

A

Total migrants = 4.5 million (1990)

EU country
Migrants from an EU country
Non EU country
Migrants from a non EU country
Total migrants into France (%) 0 5 10

0   400 km

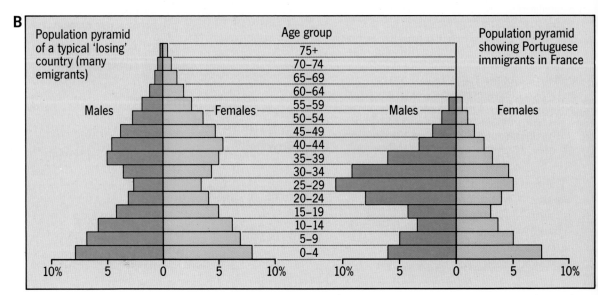

B

Population pyramid of a typical 'losing' country (many emigrants)	Age group	Population pyramid showing Portuguese immigrants in France

Males   Females   Males   Females

Age groups: 75+, 70–74, 65–69, 60–64, 55–59, 50–54, 45–49, 40–44, 35–39, 30–34, 25–29, 20–24, 15–19, 10–14, 5–9, 0–4

10% 5 0 5 10%   10% 5 0 5 10%

Conditions in France As has already been mentioned (page 60), France had a shortage of workers after the Second World War. Workers from neighbouring poorer parts of southern Europe and North Africa were encouraged to move (map **A**). The largest number of these migrants came from Portugal. Many new Portuguese arrivals initially found work on farms, but soon turned to better-paid jobs in the construction industry, factories, hotels, restaurants, etc. By French standards these jobs often demanded long unsociable working hours and were poorly paid. (photo **C**).

The migrant Portuguese could, however, earn wages as much as five times higher than those paid at home. Yet it was a sacrifice. Many had to leave their families for several months at a time. They had to live with other workers often in crowded rooms in poor quality government-built flats similar to those in photo **D**. Working conditions were often bad and a working day could last 18 hours. As France had a high standard of living, much of the money the Portuguese earned went on accommodation, transport and cheap meals. What was left over was sent home. It was little use complaining about their conditions partly because of language problems and partly because many were illegal immigrants.

The position today It is becoming harder for migrant workers to find and keep jobs, especially as it tends to be the unskilled jobs which are lost first at a time of economic recession. Bad feeling towards migrant workers and those who have brought their families with them is growing. So far most resentment has been directed at the North Africans because of differences in language, culture and religion.

C

D

Activities

1 a) Rank in order the six places from which France has received most immigrants.
   b) What do you notice about the location of these places?

2 a) If you were Portuguese give some of the
   i) reasons why you might want to go to work in France;
   ii) problems you might leave behind in Portugal.
   b) If you were French give some of the
   i) advantages of having Portuguese migrants coming to work in your country;
   ii) problems which you think the migrant workers may create.

Summary

Although the movement of workers from poorer countries to wealthier countries has many advantages, it also creates many problems.

Regional migration in the EU

Most migrations take place between different regions **within** a country. People will move away from regions which have an unfavourable natural environment and few natural resources. People will move to those regions which have a lower relief, more favourable soils and climate, a better transport system, and more raw materials and job opportunities. Two adjacent regions in southern France are the Cevennes and Languedoc-Roussillon. The Cevennes is a mountainous area from which people move. Languedoc-Roussillon has the highest immigration rate of all the regions in the EU. Landsketch **A** gives some reasons for this regional movement.

A

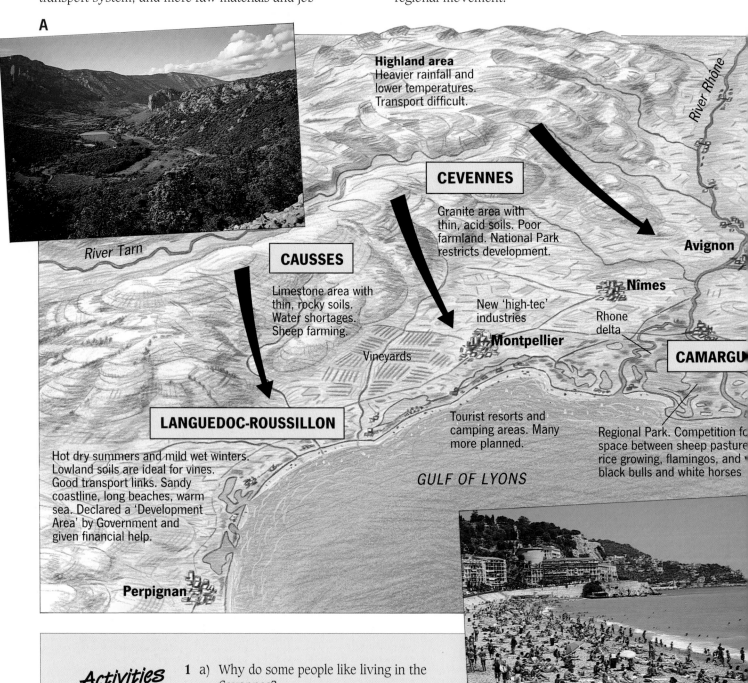

Highland area
Heavier rainfall and lower temperatures. Transport difficult.

River Rhône

CEVENNES
Granite area with thin, acid soils. Poor farmland. National Park restricts development.

Avignon

River Tarn

CAUSSES
Limestone area with thin, rocky soils. Water shortages. Sheep farming.

New 'high-tec' industries

Nîmes

Rhone delta

Vineyards

Montpellier

CAMARGU

LANGUEDOC-ROUSSILLON

Tourist resorts and camping areas. Many more planned.

Regional Park. Competition fo space between sheep pasture rice growing, flamingos, and black bulls and white horses

Hot dry summers and mild wet winters. Lowland soils are ideal for vines. Good transport links. Sandy coastline, long beaches, warm sea. Declared a 'Development Area' by Government and given financial help.

GULF OF LYONS

Perpignan

Beach at Nice, Côte d'Azur

Activities

1 a) Why do some people like living in the Cevennes?
  b) Why do other people move away from the Cevennes?
  c) Why are so many people moving into Languedoc-Roussillon?

2 What effect will these population movements have on each region?

▶ *Seasonal migration in the EU* ◀

Seasonal movement is when people move home for part of the year. Two regions in France where this occurs are the High Alps and the Camargue-Côte d'Azur (map **B**). For many centuries farmers in this area have taken their sheep from winter pastures in the flat Camargue district of the Rhône delta to summer pastures in the High Alps. Although this type of farming, known as **transhumance**, is dying out, it is being replaced by another type of seasonal movement - tourism. In winter the snow of the High Alps attracts many skiers. In summer it is the hot, dry weather of the Côte d'Azur which becomes the magnet for many visitors. Landsketch **B** gives some reasons for these seasonal movements.

B

River Durance

HIGH ALPS

Ski-ing in winter. New resorts are using up sheep pastures. Some tourists in summer. New roads have been built.

In June sheep are taken to Alpine pastures. Originally this was a month's walk, but sheep are now moved in double-decker lorries. Lorries cause congestion on narrow roads twice a year. Transhumance is in decline and pastures are being lost. Rural areas are too isolated for young people and there are better-paid jobs in the cities.

DURANCE VALLEY

Nice

In October sheep are brought down to the Camargue. It has mild, wet winters which are good for grass. The land is flat and there are few tourists. Summers are too hot and dry for grass to grow.

Cannes

COTE D'AZUR

Marseille

Toulon

Rocky headlands.
Sandy or rocky beaches.
Hot, dry summers.
Good harbours.
Large hotels and restaurants.

Activities

1 a) What is transhumance?
   b) Why are sheep taken to the Camargue in winter and to the High Alps in summer?
   c) Why do so many people visit the High Alps in winter?
   d) Why do so many people visit the Côte d'Azur in summer?

2 What effect will these seasonal movements have upon each of the two regions?

Summary

Whether or not migration is between countries, between regions or at different times of the year, it has considerable effects upon the different regions involved.

▶ *What are the alternative policies to migration in the EU?* ◀

The United Nations (UN) claim that '80 million people have left their homes for economic, political, environmental or other reasons - often embarking on precarious new lives'. Although the vast majority of these moves have been made in and between developing countries, the EU now has eight million immigrants, a number which is growing rapidly.

Migrants into the EU

Most early arrivals were **economic migrants**. These were people looking for work in the hope of improving their standard of living, e.g. North Africans moving to France and Turks moving to West Germany. Many more recent migrants have been seeking asylum (safety). If asylum-seekers can prove that they are escaping from political, racial or religious persecution at home then they are granted the uncertain status of being **refugees** (e.g. Bosnians into Germany). The UN define people who are forced to move within their home country as **displaced persons** (e.g. ethnic cleansing in the former Yugoslavia). The largest proportion of migrants today are **illegal immigrants** who enter a country without permission (e.g. West Africans dropped in the sea two or three kilometres off the coast of Italy or Spain, who then try to swim ashore).

Until the 1990s most EU countries had a fairly liberal policy on immigration. However, there is a changing attitude amongst Community members for several reasons.

- Growing numbers of immigrants from eastern Europe and the CIS (one estimate suggests that another four million could move to the west by 1995).
- Fears that immigrants pose a domestic threat (extracts **A** and **B**).
- Increasing numbers of illegal immigrants.

Some of these views and changes in legislation are expressed in diagram **C**.

A

Turks in Germany

January, 1993

A Turkish spokesperson said, 'We have lived here for years yet we are still without representation and feel cut off from German life. We are seen as aliens which makes us an easy target. Germans have a negative attitude to people who look and think differently.' In reply a German claimed, 'Some Turks may have lived here since arriving as "guest workers" in the 1960s but only 1 per cent have taken out German citizenship. They refuse to apply as it would mean giving up Turkish nationality. They do not want to be German.'

In the boom years of the 1960s and 1970s, the lack of political rights was, in the eyes of most Turks, compensated by relatively good wages. Even if they were not treated as equals, the Turks were tolerated by most West Germans who recognised that they did the menial jobs they themselves would not do. Since the economic problems resulting from German re-unification, the Turks have been increasingly lumped with asylum-seekers and other refugees and accused of draining resources and 'taking' jobs. Groups of extremists have burnt Turkish property and have been responsible for several murders. In response the majority of Germans have reacted with large anti-racist marches.

B

November, 1992

North Africans in France

Until recently North African migrants, though never encouraged to integrate socially, existed peacefully with the French and tensions were few. However, as unemployment has continued to rise then accusations have been made that the North Africans are taking jobs from the French. They are also feared for their very high birth rate and their alien customs. Muslim extremists have encouraged strikes of Arab workers and discouraged young women and new immigrants from adopting French customs. Trouble finally broke out in several large urban areas. Here the immigrants live in high-rise ghettos where they are shunned and despised by the French. Race riots and the growth of an extreme French racist political party has shocked many young French people into launching a campaign of support and solidarity for the young North Africans in their country.

C

United Kingdom: We have a quota system which restricts entry to a proportion of people from various countries but it is weighed against New Commonwealth immigrants. We will allow genuine refugees from places like Bosnia to enter if they can prove that their lives would be in danger if they were sent home – but not economic migrants just wanting jobs. Those refugees we do accept may be sent to 'quieter' parts of Britain like Cumbria. We fine airlines that bring in people without a valid passport or entry visa. We are also worried about the abolition of border controls between EU countries – it could let in terrorists and drug dealers.

France: Since 1974 only those rejoining their families have been allowed entry. We offered money to migrants to tempt them to be repatriated. Very few accepted and some who did just took the money, went home and then returned! We are now being swamped by illegal immigrants or those who come with 'tourist visas' and stay. In future migrants will get a 'transit (passing through) visa'.

EU IMMIGRATION POLICY GROUP

Italy: As so many Italians have emigrated it was right that we, in return, allowed free entry to all immigrants. But we have had so many problems with refugees and illegal immigrants that people from North Africa and Turkey will only be admitted if they have a valid passport.

EU Commissioner: We must try to halt illegal immigration; plan legal immigration; help the social integration of future immigrants. We may have to restrict entry to people with certain skills which are lacking in the EC.

Germany: We have had an open door policy to all migrants. However, since accepting nearly 2 million ethnic Germans from Eastern Europe and the CIS, and 0.6 million legal refugees from the former Yugoslavia, we are having to revise our ideas. Many Germans feel we have already accepted too many.

Activities

1 What is the difference between economic migrants, refugees and illegal immigrants?

2 Why is the increase in population movement into the EU causing concern among several member countries?

3 a) Why are individual EU countries such as Britain, France, Germany and Italy looking for new immigration policies with stricter controls?

   b) Why is it important for the EU to have a common immigration policy?

   c) What do you think the EU's policy towards immigration should be?

Summary

As the number of migrants, both legal and illegal, into the EU increases, individual governments are changing their policies and putting pressure on the EU itself to produce a 'common' immigration policy.

▶ What gives France its sense of identity? ◀

France was, until the re-unification of Germany in 1991, the largest country in the European Union (EU). Its area is just over twice the size of the UK.

Physical (map A)

The northern half of France consists of low-lying plains with, to the east of Paris, a series of chalk and limestone ridges (escarpments) separated by clay vales. Across central parts of the country are several areas of low mountains which include the Massif Central and the Vosges. To the south, the land rises up to the mountainous areas of the Pyrenees, in the south-west, and the Alps, in the south-east. Four large rivers and their tributaries drain most of the country. The Rhône flows southwards, entering the Mediterranean Sea by a delta. The Garonne and Loire both flow westwards into the Bay of Biscay, and the Seine flows north-westwards into the English Channel. A section of one of Europe's largest rivers, the Rhine, forms part of France's eastern border.

Climate (map B)

Climate is the term used to describe the average weather conditions of a place. Travelling southwards in France the weather gets warmer, sunnier and drier. The weather in the west of France, which is nearer to the sea, is warmer in winter, cooler in summer and receives more rainfall than places inland and to the east.

A

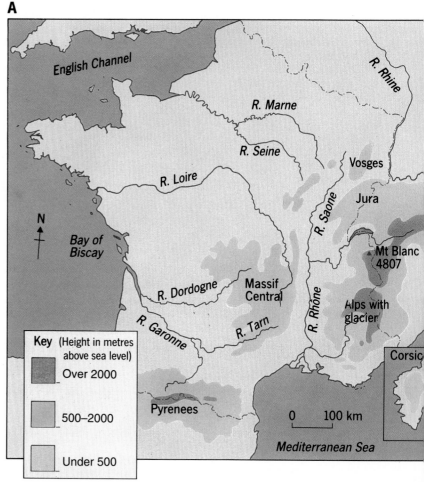

Key (Height in metres above sea level)
- Over 2000
- 500–2000
- Under 500

B

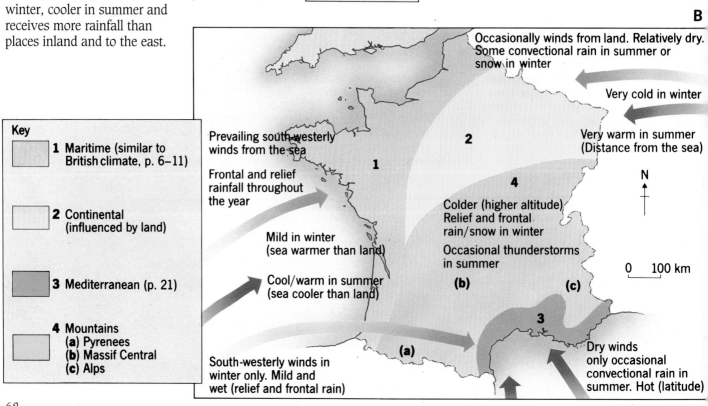

Key
- **1 Maritime** (similar to British climate, p. 6–11)
- **2 Continental** (influenced by land)
- **3 Mediterranean** (p. 21)
- **4 Mountains**
  - **(a)** Pyrenees
  - **(b)** Massif Central
  - **(c)** Alps

Distribution of population (map C)

France has a total population of 55 million people, about one million less than that of the UK. However, as France has twice the area of the UK this means that its population is far more spread out (map **C**) and its population density is only half that of the UK. The greatest concentration is in Paris where one person out of every seven of the total French population lives. The next highest concentrations are the coastal areas and along the valleys of the main rivers. The areas where fewest people live tend to be those at higher altitudes (compare maps **A** and **C**), although some of the higher alpine areas do have an average population density due to winter sports and the availability of hydro-electricity for modern high-tech industry. Seventy four per cent of France's total population live in urban areas.

Different groups of people tend to develop their own customs and way of life. This can include their language and religion, how they dress and behave, what they eat and drink, and what they do in their spare time. This helps to create a national sense of identity. If we put these characteristics together for France we get a mental picture of typical, or stereotype, French people. There is a danger in compiling stereotypes, however, and we must remember that French people are individuals with each person being different to the next.

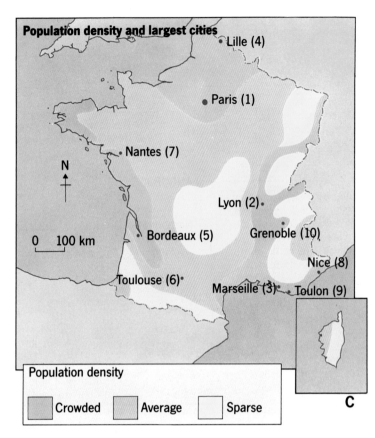

Population density and largest cities

- Lille (4)
- Paris (1)
- Nantes (7)
- Lyon (2)
- Bordeaux (5)
- Grenoble (10)
- Nice (8)
- Toulouse (6)
- Marseille (3)
- Toulon (9)

N↑

0   100 km

Population density

| Crowded | Average | Sparse |

C

Activities

1 a) How is the climate of France affected by the following factors?
   - Latitude
   - Distance from the sea
   - Prevailing winds
   - Altitude
   b) Which parts of France (give compass directions) are most likely to receive
   i) relief and frontal rain throughout the year,
   ii) convectional rain in summer,
   iii) a summer drought,
   iv) heavy snowfalls in winter?

2 a) Re-write the following passage choosing the correct word or figure from the pairs in brackets.

> France has an area of 550 000 km² and a population of (55/250) million people. This means it has a population density of (200/100) people per km². One in seven of the French population live in (urban areas/Paris) and 74 per cent live in (rural/urban) areas. The highest concentrations are (along coasts/inland) and in (mountains/river valleys).

b) The last paragraph on this page begins with 'Different groups of people tend to develop their own customs and way of life'. For the majority of French people:
   i) What is their religion?
   ii) What do they like to eat and to drink?
   iii) How do they like to dress?
   iv) What do they like to do in their spare time?
c) i) What is a stereotype?
   ii) Why is it wrong to talk about a French stereotype?

3 Name the places referred to on map **D**.

D

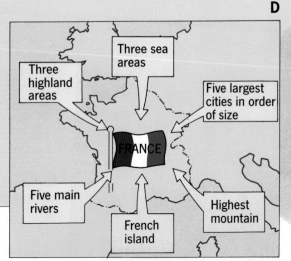

- Three sea areas
- Three highland areas
- Five largest cities in order of size
- Five main rivers
- Highest mountain
- French island
- FRANCE

Summary

There are distinctive physical and climatic regions within France. Differences in relief and climate influence the distribution of population. Each country develops its own customs and way of life and these combine to give that country its own sense of identity.

69

▶ *How does the environment affect land use and settlement?* ◀

A Land use, occupations and settlement in 1960

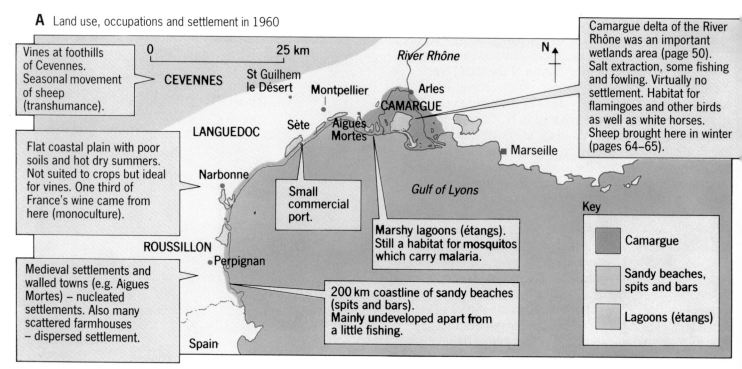

Vines at foothills of Cevennes. Seasonal movement of sheep (transhumance).

Flat coastal plain with poor soils and hot dry summers. Not suited to crops but ideal for vines. One third of France's wine came from here (monoculture).

Medieval settlements and walled towns (e.g. Aigues Mortes) – nucleated settlements. Also many scattered farmhouses – dispersed settlement.

Small commercial port.

Marshy lagoons (étangs). Still a habitat for mosquitos which carry malaria.

200 km coastline of sandy beaches (spits and bars). Mainly undeveloped apart from a little fishing.

Camargue delta of the River Rhône was an important wetlands area (page 50). Salt extraction, some fishing and fowling. Virtually no settlement. Habitat for flamingoes and other birds as well as white horses. Sheep brought here in winter (pages 64–65).

Key

Camargue

Sandy beaches, spits and bars

Lagoons (étangs)

The land use, occupations and settlement patterns of an area are often a response to such environmental factors as the climate, soils and relief of that area. This can be illustrated by that part of South-west France which extends eastwards from the Spanish border, through the provinces of Roussillon and Languedoc, to the Rhône Delta (the Camargue). In 1960 this region (map **A**) had one of the lowest standards of living in France. It had relatively few jobs, poor communications, an inefficient water supply, and a lack of services and basic amenities. Most jobs were connected with agriculture. However, the hot, dry summers and poor soils meant that only vines could be grown successfully. The growing of a single crop is called **monoculture** (photos **B** and **C**).

The French government saw the need to improve the standard of living in the region. They tried to do this through developments in farming, communications and tourism.

- Farming has been improved and diversified by constructing canals to divert water from main rivers such as the Rhône. Irrigation channels take the water to individual farms and fields, allowing fruit and vegetables to be grown on a commercial scale.
- Communications have been improved by building an autoroute (motorway) and laying track for the TGV.
- Tourism was seen as the major potential in the region. New purpose holiday resorts were built with the hope of attracting visitors from foreign countries and encouraging French people to take their holidays in France rather than to spend their money in other countries. La Grande Motte was the first government financed resort. It initially provided 45 000 rooms as well as sites for camping and caravans. However, despite its excellent beach and tourist facilities, it does not blend in with the environment (photo **E**). More recent resorts consist of low-rise villas such as Le Cap d'Agde, but these resorts tend to be more spread out and lack a central focal point.

Map **D** shows how land use, occupations and settlement patterns had altered by the early 1990s.

B Traditional farming Languedoc

C The village of St Guilhem le Désert

Deserted farmhouses have become second homes. One in nine French families have second homes (one in 200 in the UK).

Montpellier has become a major centre for new high-tech industries. Based on excellent communications and the climate.

CEVENNES

River Rhône

Arles

Montpellier

La Grande Motte

Improved communications TGV railway (1993); A9 autoroute (motorway); airport

Marseille

	Camargue (Regional Wildlife Park)
	Irrigated areas
	Tourist areas
- - -	TGV railway (1993); A9 (motorway)

Irrigation canals from the Rhône and rivers in the Cevennes have turned many vine-growing areas into commercial fruit and vegetable farms

Sète

Le Cap d'Agde

Narbonne

Gruissan-Place

Malarial marshes drained. Now used for oyster and mussel farms

Port Leucate

Perpignan

St Cyprien

New resorts along coast from linear settlements

Spain

Wetland areas were under threat from irrigation (for rice growing), drainage (to provide grazing for animals), industry, housing, salt extraction. Large areas have been made a Regional Park. Less winter grazing by sheep.

D Land use, occupations and settlement in the early 1990s

Newer purpose-built resorts to west blend in better with the environment

Tourist centres were created. The first was a purpose-built complex at La Grande Motte. It has excellent beaches, first class marinas and plenty of tourist amenities but the resort is an eyesore (photo E). Water pollution from sewage and oil is a problem. There are many jobs in summer but few in winter.

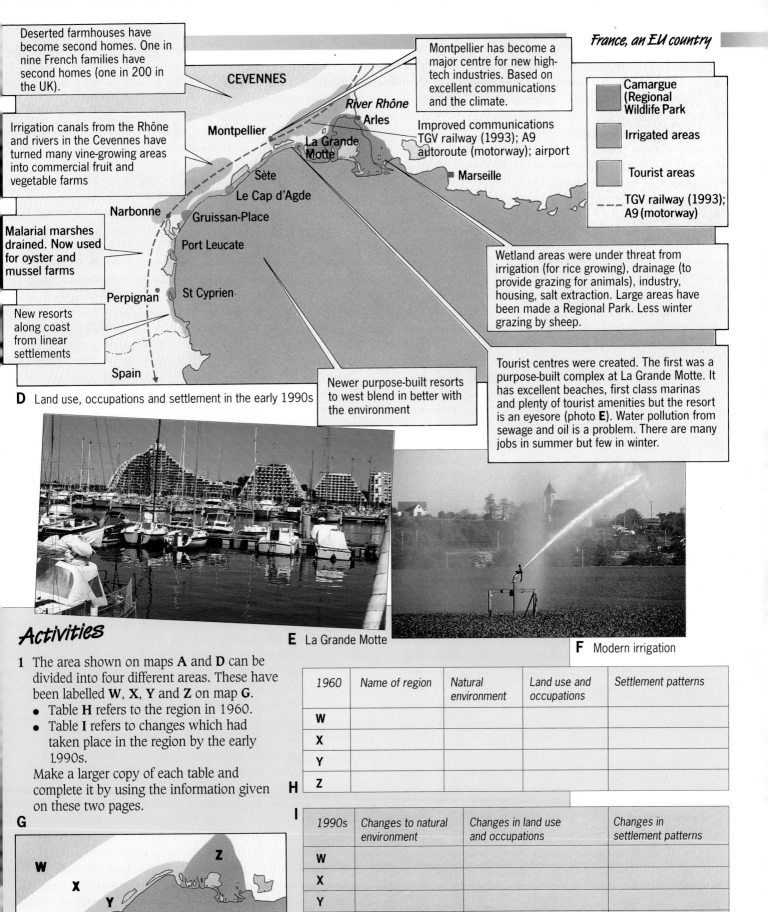

E La Grande Motte

F Modern irrigation

Activities

1 The area shown on maps **A** and **D** can be divided into four different areas. These have been labelled **W**, **X**, **Y** and **Z** on map **G**.
   - Table **H** refers to the region in 1960.
   - Table **I** refers to changes which had taken place in the region by the early 1990s.

   Make a larger copy of each table and complete it by using the information given on these two pages.

G

W

Z

X

Y

1960	Name of region	Natural environment	Land use and occupations	Settlement patterns
W				
X				
Y				
H Z				

1990s	Changes to natural environment	Changes in land use and occupations	Changes in settlement patterns
W			
X			
Y			
I Z			

Summary The main types of land use, occupations and settlement patterns of an area can often be explained by its environment.

▶ *What are the main regions in France?* ◀

What is a region? A region is an area of land which has common characteristics. It is therefore different to other regions. Different people, using maps for different purposes, can show different types of region. There is no single correct map or interpretation. Regions can be large or small, physical or human and economic.

- Physical regions are places which have similar relief (map **A**, page 68), climate (map **D**, page 23; map **B**, page 68), vegetation and soil.

- Human and economic regions include political areas (maps showing the countries of the world or the EU), population distribution (map **C**, page 69) and places with similar economic activities (farming regions or, as in map **B** below, holiday regions).

A

C

D

B Holiday regions in France

English Channel

N

2
North-east France

11b
Normandy

1 ●Paris
Ile de France

3
Lorraine and
Alsace

11a
Brittany

10
Loire Valley

4a
Jura

6
Rhône
Valley

*Bay of
Biscay*

9
Aquitaine
and the
Atlantic coast

8
Dordogne
and the
Massif Central

4b
Alps

and
Delta

5a Côte d'Azur

5b
Languedoc-
Roussillon

7 Pyrenees

Mediterranean Sea

12
Corsica

E

F

Map reference	Region	Description	Photo reference	Page reference
①	Ile de France	Cultural, religious and historic city of Paris; Versailles Palace; nightlife; EuroDisney	**A**	74, 77
②	North-east France	Vineyards of Champagne; day visits (shopping) from UK		
③	Alsace and Lorraine	Wooded hills; Rhine River cruises; castles; vineyards	**G**	
④	a) Jura	Wooded mountains; quiet villages		
	b) Alps	Winter sports; climbing/ walking in summer; spectacular scenery	**H**	56-7, 65
⑤	a) Côte d'Azur	Expensive resorts, hotels, marinas; Roman remains; headlands and bays		64, 79
	b) Languedoc-Roussillon	Sandy beaches, marinas; camping/ caravan sites; historic sites		64, 70
⑥	Rhône Valley	Historic settlements (e.g. Avignon); Camargue Regional Park		51, 71
⑦	Pyrenees	Rugged mountains, winter sports		
⑧	Dordogne/ Massif Central	Le Puy volcano National Park; limestone gorges, caves; Lascaux cave paintings; Lourdes (religious site)	**E**	
⑨	Aquitaine	Wine growing area; sand dune coast and sandy beaches; camping		
⑩	Loire Valley	Numerous châteaux (castles); river valley	**D**	
⑪	a) Brittany	Own language (Breton) and culture; scenic coast, headlands, sandy bays		
	b) Normandy	Scenic coast; quiet villages; Bayeux Tapestry; Mont St Michel	**C**	
⑫	Corsica	Rocky, scenic, unspoilt island with quiet bays and woodland		

G

H

Activities

1. a) What is a region?
   b) What is the difference between a physical and a political region?

2. Which region, or regions, would you visit in France if you wanted to:
   a) Visit art museums,
   b) Ski,
   c) See the remains of volcanoes,
   d) Sunbathe on a sandy beach,
   e) Climb mountains,
   f) Explore underground caves,
   g) Enjoy nightlife,
   h) Take part in water sports,
   i) See quiet villages,
   j) Visit historic buildings,
   k) Cruise down a river,
   l) Visit chateaux,
   m) Visit an abbey at low tide,
   n) See vineyards,
   o) Visit a Disney theme park,
   p) Camp,
   q) Make a religious pilgrimage?

3. Which of the tourist regions shown on map **A** would you most like to visit? Give reasons for your answer.

Summary

A region is an area of land which has similar characteristics. These characteristics, which can be physical or human and economic, make one region different to other regions.

▶ What are the physical differences between the Ile de France and Provence?

Landscape

The **Ile de France** lies in a low-lying basin (map **A**, page 72). It is drained by several meandering rivers which include the Seine, the Marne and the Oise. Much of the underlying rock is limestone with, in places, sandstone. As these rocks are pervious it should mean that rainwater can easily infiltrate into the ground to leave the surface relatively dry. In many places the rock has been covered either by gravels, sands and silt deposited by rivers during times of flood, or by a layer of clay. The resultant differences between rock and soil types has created a range of contrasting local landscapes which are known to the French as **'pays'**. The edges of the Ile de France are ringed with extensive areas of natural beech and oak forest, e.g. Fontainebleau (photo **A**). These forests are referred to as the 'lungs of Paris' as they clean the air of the industrial city (page 42). Poplar trees have also been allowed to grow since they act as windbreaks and reduce the force of the wind.

Provence (map **A**, page 72) can be divided into three main physical areas. In the extreme west is the valley of the River Rhône with its fertile flood plain and its marshy delta (the Camargue – pages 70 to 71). The coast, from east of the delta to the Italian border, is called the Côte d'Azur. It is indented and becomes increasingly rugged towards the east. Tall headlands, formed where the Alps reach down to the sea, are separated by sandy beaches and rocky inlets. Small islands and the blue (azure) sea and sky add to the area's scenic attraction. Inland from the coast rise the Alpes-Maritime (Maritime Alps) and, beyond them, the Hautes-Alpes (High Alps). The Hautes-Alpes are snow-covered for several months in winter. Rivers, such as the Durance and the Var, have a high discharge following the snow melt. The extra energy which they have at this time has cut deep gorge-like valleys through the mountains. Away from the Rhône Valley much of the region has thin soils and is covered by either remnants of Mediterranean woodland or areas of maquis and garrigue scrubland (page 36).

A Fontainebleau Forest, Ile de France

B Provence

Activities

1 Describe the main physical differences between the Ile de France and Provence. Give your answer under the following headings:
   - Relief
   - Rivers
   - Soils
   - Vegetation.

2 Draw two labelled landsketches of photos **A** and **B**. On each, label at least four physical points to show differences between the two regions.

Climate

The climate of the **Ile de France** is very similar to that experienced in the south-east of England. It has cool winters and warm summers (graph **C**) with prevailing south-westerly winds which blow from the Atlantic Ocean. Although these winds give rainfall throughout the year, annual totals are not particularly high. When winds do blow from the land they are likely to bring cold, dry weather with a risk of snow in winter and very warm, dry conditions, with the chance of convectional thunderstorms, in summer (map **B**, page 68). The region does not experience any particular climatic hazard.

Provence, although only some 350 km to the south, has a very different type of climate to that of the Ile de France (graph **D**). It has hot, dry summers, when the wind tends to blow from Africa and the Sahara Desert, and mild, wet winters, when the wind changes direction and comes from the Atlantic Ocean. Before the Second World War the Côte d'Azur was the most popular location in the world for people wanting to take a winter holiday. Since then, although it has maintained its popularity as a holiday area, the majority of tourists now arrive during the summer months. They want to take advantage of the climate and its almost guaranteed long hours of unbroken sunshine and high temperatures. The region does, however, experience two climatic hazards.

- The heat and drought of summer can cause water shortages and provides ideal conditions for forest fires.
- The Mistral, a very strong wind originating in the Alps, can give cold and stormy conditions in the Rhône delta as it is channelled down the Rhône Valley.

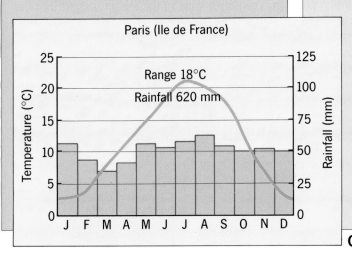

Paris (Ile de France)
Range 18°C
Rainfall 620 mm

C

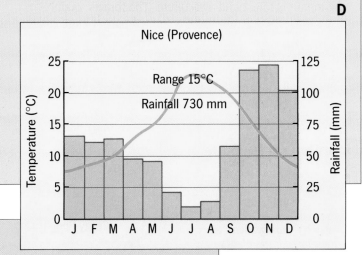

Nice (Provence)
Range 15°C
Rainfall 730 mm

D

Activities

3 Make a copy of table **E** and complete it as follows.
   a) Use graphs **C** and **D** to give actual climate figures.
   b) Use information from these two pages, and pages 8 to 11, 21 and 68 to explain the differences in the figures between the Ile de France and Provence.

4 Make a copy of map **F**. Add the two correct descriptions by choosing the correct word or phrase from the pair in brackets to show how the climate changes as you move north or south in France.

E

	Ile de France	Provence	Reasons for difference
July temperature (°C)			
January temperature (°C)			
Annual temperature range (°C)			
Total rainfall (mm)			
Seasonal distribution of rainfall			
Climatic hazards			

Winters get (colder/milder)
Summers are (hotter/cooler)
Rainfall (decreases/increases) and falls (all year/only in winter)
Climate hazards (include strong winds/none)

Winters get (colder/milder)
Summers are (hotter/cooler)
Rainfall (decreases/increases) and falls (all year/only in winter)
Climate hazards (include strong winds/none)

F

Summary

There are considerable differences in both the landscape (relief, drainage, soils and natural vegetation) and climate between the Ile de France and Provence.

▶ What are the land use and main occupations in the Ile de France? ◀

The Ile de France is the third smallest in area out of France's 22 political regions. However, with a population of 10.6 million, it has the country's highest population density (diagram **A**). Almost one-fifth of the total French population live in this region, which includes the city of Paris.

Land use

The central part of the Ile de France consists of the urban area of Paris which is continuously taking up larger amounts of land. Apart from the expansion of the city itself and the creation of five new towns (map **B**), many outlying villages are becoming increasingly suburbanised. These settlements are linked to Paris by an increasing number of major roads and railways. The major land use for most of the remainder of the region is forest and agriculture. The forests, mainly natural beech and oak, initially formed part of large estates (e.g. Fontainebleau and the Chevreuse Valley). They are now protected by the state and provide places of recreation for urban dwellers. Agriculture is both intensive and commercial. Surrounding Paris are numerous smallholdings providing fresh market

A

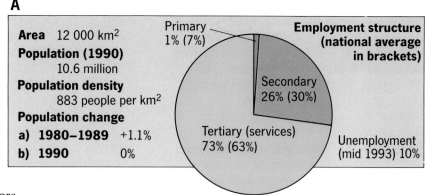

Area	12 000 km^2
Population (1990)	10.6 million
Population density	883 people per km^2

Population change
a) **1980–1989** +1.1%
b) **1990** 0%

Employment structure (national average in brackets)
Primary 1% (7%)
Secondary 26% (30%)
Tertiary (services) 73% (63%)
Unemployment (mid 1993) 10%

garden produce. The south-west of the region merges into the wheat-growing area of Beauce. Between the rivers Seine and Marne is the dairy farming 'pays' (district) of Brie, which gives its name to an internationally well-known cheese.

The employment structure for the region shows that most people work in either the secondary or tertiary sectors (diagram **A**). The vast majority of these jobs are found within Paris itself (map **B**).

B

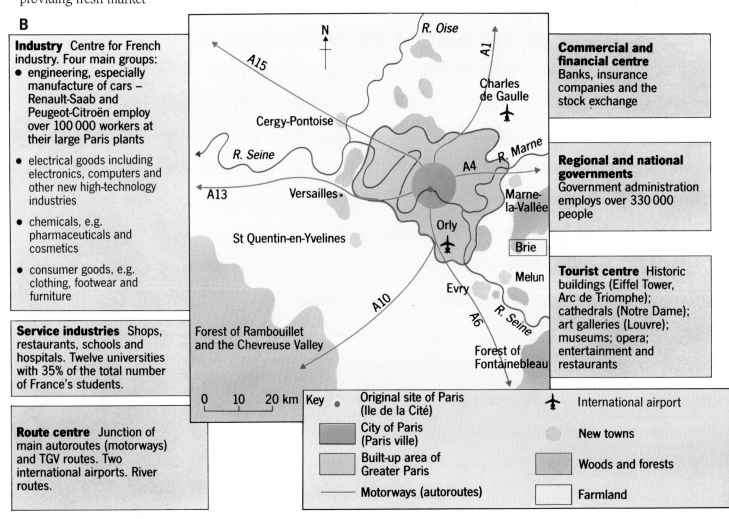

Industry Centre for French industry. Four main groups:
- engineering, especially manufacture of cars – Renault-Saab and Peugeot-Citroën employ over 100 000 workers at their large Paris plants
- electrical goods including electronics, computers and other new high-technology industries
- chemicals, e.g. pharmaceuticals and cosmetics
- consumer goods, e.g. clothing, footwear and furniture

Service industries Shops, restaurants, schools and hospitals. Twelve universities with 35% of the total number of France's students.

Route centre Junction of main autoroutes (motorways) and TGV routes. Two international airports. River routes.

Commercial and financial centre Banks, insurance companies and the stock exchange

Regional and national governments Government administration employs over 330 000 people

Tourist centre Historic buildings (Eiffel Tower, Arc de Triomphe); cathedrals (Notre Dame); art galleries (Louvre); museums; opera; entertainment and restaurants

Map labels: R. Oise, A1, A15, Charles de Gaulle, Cergy-Pontoise, R. Seine, R. Marne, A4, A13, Versailles, Marne-la-Vallée, Orly, Brie, St Quentin-en-Yvelines, Melun, Evry, A10, R. Seine, A6, Forest of Rambouillet and the Chevreuse Valley, Forest of Fontainebleau

Scale: 0 10 20 km

Key
- Original site of Paris (Ile de la Cité)
- City of Paris (Paris ville)
- Built-up area of Greater Paris
- Motorways (autoroutes)
- ✈ International airport
- New towns
- Woods and forests
- Farmland

Settlement

Most of the settlements, including Paris and its new towns, are nucleated. A more linear pattern of settlement, inhabited by commuters, has developed along many of the main roads which lead into the capital. Many younger people still migrate to Paris. This is because the city, being the capital and industrial centre of the country, offers the best career opportunities as well as providing the most and the best-paid jobs. However, an almost equal number of people are moving out of the city to try to escape from the problems of overcrowding, traffic congestion, high land prices, and air and noise pollution. Although attempts have been made to create jobs in the new towns, many people still have to commute to Paris for work.

D Aerial view of Paris

C Palace of Versailles

Activities

1 a) What proportion of people living in the Ile de France are employed in each of the primary, secondary and tertiary sectors?
  b) What are the three main types of land use in the Ile de France?

2 a) What are the main types of primary activity in the Ile de France?
  b) What are the main types of secondary activity (industry) found in Paris?
  c) Why does Paris have a high percentage of tertiary (service) jobs?

3 Map **E** is a Landsat photo of the Ile de France. It covers the same area as that shown on map **B**. Using the photo and the map, name the following:
  a) Rivers ①, ② and ③.
  b) Urban area ④.
  c) New towns ⑤, ⑥, ⑦, ⑧ and ⑨.
  d) Airports ⑩ and ⑪.
  e) Forest areas ⑫ and ⑬.
  f) The economic activity shown by the pinkish/red areas.

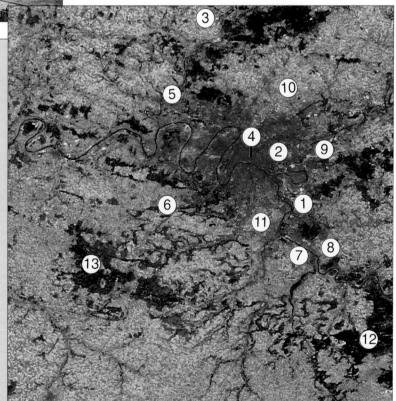

E

Summary

The Ile de France is the richest and most densely populated region in France. Paris and its surrounding towns cover much of the land. Most of the remainder is either left as forest or is used for farming.

▶ *What are the land use and main occupations in Provence?* ◀

Provence is the seventh largest in area out of France's 22 political regions. With a population of 4.2 million, it has the sixth largest population density in the country (diagram **A**). Compared with the Ile de France, Provence is two and a half times larger in area, but has a population density two and a half times less. The region has, after Languedoc-Roussillon, the fastest population growth rate in France.

Land use

The lower Rhône Valley and parts of the Mediterranean coast have the highest population density in Provence (map **B**). Consequently more of the land is used for settlement in these parts than elsewhere in the region. The often narrow valley floor of the Rhône provides a natural route for rail and motorways which link the north and south of France.

The major land use throughout Provence is agriculture. The floor of the Rhône Valley is important for market gardening, the valley sides for vines and the delta for rice. Away from the Rhône, vines and olives are more important towards the south and west of the region, and citrus fruits along the coast towards the east. The initial cultivation of aromatic Mediterranean plants (page 36) such as lavender, rosemary, jasmine and roses led to the growth of the perfume industry. Today, many of these plants are grown for the cut-flower market. Higher up in the Alps there has been a decline in animal rearing and in the seasonal movement of sheep and goats (transhumance – page 65). The land is still left as

A

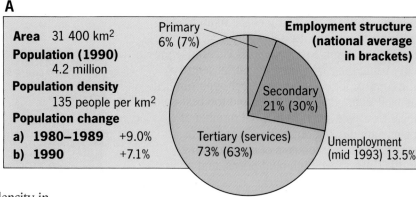

| Area 31 400 km² |
| Population (1990) 4.2 million |
| Population density 135 people per km² |
| Population change |
| a) 1980–1989 +9.0% |
| b) 1990 +7.1% |

Employment structure (national average in brackets): Primary 6% (7%), Secondary 21% (30%), Tertiary (services) 73% (63%), Unemployment (mid 1993) 13.5%

forest or scrubland in the higher, less accessible areas while reservoirs cover parts of the Durance and Verdon valleys. There are four National Parks in the region, including the Camargue (page 71).

The only place where industry becomes a major land use is in the old seaport of Marseille and around the new port of Fos. Fos has large oil refineries, steel and petrochemical works and Europe's largest helicopter factory. Mainly due to its attractive scenery and climate, parts of the Côte d'Azur between Cannes and Nice have become important for high-technology industries and research (e.g. Sophia-Antipolis International Science Park).

The employment structure for the region shows that most people are engaged in the tertiary sector (diagram **A**). The local economy is based on farming (primary), tourism (tertiary) and, increasingly, high-tech industry (secondary).

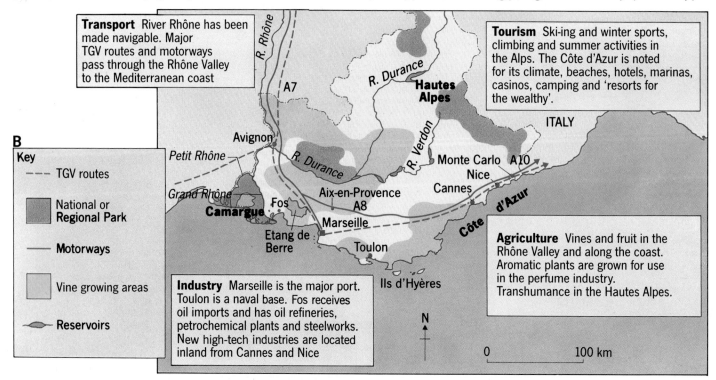

B

Transport River Rhône has been made navigable. Major TGV routes and motorways pass through the Rhône Valley to the Mediterranean coast

Tourism Ski-ing and winter sports, climbing and summer activities in the Alps. The Côte d'Azur is noted for its climate, beaches, hotels, marinas, casinos, camping and 'resorts for the wealthy'.

Key
- --- TGV routes
- National or Regional Park
- Motorways
- Vine growing areas
- Reservoirs

Industry Marseille is the major port. Toulon is a naval base. Fos receives oil imports and has oil refineries, petrochemical plants and steelworks. New high-tech industries are located inland from Cannes and Nice

Agriculture Vines and fruit in the Rhône Valley and along the coast. Aromatic plants are grown for use in the perfume industry. Transhumance in the Hautes Alpes.

0 100 km

Settlement

As many of the settlements are old in origin, they were forced to develop a defensive nucleated pattern as protection against attack by invaders (photo **C**). Tourist resorts along the Mediterranean coast have also often developed a nucleated shape, this time due to the limited amounts of lowland upon which to build and expand (photo **D**). Between the resorts, villas and other expensive property extend in a linear pattern around the many headlands. In more Alpine areas, the settlement pattern is one of dispersed farms. During the early part of this century many of Provence's fortified hilltop villages and individual farms had become increasingly deserted as people moved to the towns (rural depopulation). More recently many houses in these villages, together with outlying farms, have been bought and renovated, mainly by Parisians, for use as second homes or for retirement.

Modern developments, as elsewhere in the world, create problems as well as bring advantages. Local people do not always appreciate the changed character of their villages, nor can they compete with outsiders willing to pay inflated house prices. Tourists arriving in mid-summer block local roads while a proposed second TGV route, aimed at reducing overcrowding on the railway, has been violently opposed by local people not wishing to see more vineyards and forest destroyed.

C Gordes, Provence

D City and resort of Nice

Activities

1 a) What proportion of people living in Provence are employed in each of the primary, secondary and tertiary sectors?
   b) What are the main types of land use in Provence?

2 a) What are the main types of primary activity in Provence?
   b) What are the main types of secondary activity (industry) found in Provence?
   c) Why does the Côte d'Azur have a high percentage of tertiary (service) jobs?

3 Photo **E** was taken on the coast of Provence. Draw a landsketch of the photo and on it add labels to show different types of:
   ● Settlement
   ● Land use
   ● Employment

E

Summary

Parts of Provence are amongst the wealthiest and most densely populated in France. Much of the land is either left as forest and scrub or is used for farming. Built up areas are mainly confined to parts of the Rhône Valley and the Mediterranean coast.

8 The USA, a developed country
▶ What are the general features of the USA, CIS and Japan? ◀

Location (map A)
The USA, CIS and Japan are all located north of the Equator lying mainly between the Tropic of Cancer and the Arctic Circle.

Physical features (map A)
Japan, western USA and the east of the CIS all border the Pacific Ocean. Places surrounding the Pacific Ocean are located on plate boundaries where there are high mountains, active volcanoes and frequent, often severe, earthquakes. The south of the CIS also has high mountains and experiences strong earthquakes. In comparison, central parts of the USA and the CIS are away from plate boundaries. Here the land is usually flat, low-lying and forms part of extensive river drainage basins. In these drainage basins, large rivers meander across wide flood plains. The rivers in Japan, in contrast, are short and fast flowing.

Area and population (diagram B)
The maps in diagram **B** are called **topological maps**. They are a simple, visual method of showing information and in doing so they make it easier to make comparisons between places. In the first map the area of each country is drawn to scale but its shape is distorted and distances and directions are inaccurate. The size of the country in the remaining maps is based either upon its total population or its population density.

A

ARCTIC OCEAN

ALASKA — Arctic Circle 66½°N

▲ Mt McKinley 6194

E

Lake Superior

Mt St Helens ▲

ROCKIES

San Francisco **E**

R Colorado R Mississippi-Missouri

USA

E

PACIFIC OCEAN

ATLANTIC OCEA

HAWAII — Tropic of Cancer 23½°N

160°W ▲ Mauna Loa

120°W

60°W

Economic activities and trade (table C)
The USA and Japan are two very industrialised and wealthy countries. They are the world leaders in producing high-technology products such as cars and electrical goods. Much of their wealth has come from selling these products to other countries. The CIS is also industrialised, but its factories are less modern than those of the USA and Japan. As a result it produces goods which are fewer in quantity and poorer in quality than those of the other two countries. Table **C** uses statistics to summarise the trade of the three countries. It lists the major exports and imports of each country as well as showing their main trade links.

B

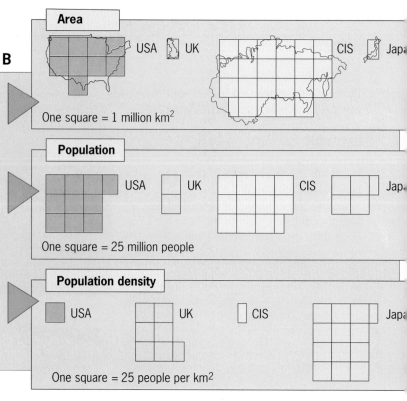

Area

USA   UK   CIS   Japa

One square = 1 million km²

Population

USA   UK   CIS   Jap

One square = 25 million people

Population density

USA   UK   CIS   Japa

One square = 25 people per km²

Look at the first map. By counting the number of squares you can work out the approximate **area** of each country. Based on area the CIS is the largest country in the world. The USA is the fourth largest country in the world. The UK, which has been added for interest, and Japan, are by comparison very small.

When looking at the total **populations** of the four countries, the CIS is still the largest, closely followed by the USA. However, the difference between them is much less than it was when comparing their areas.

Population density is a measure of how crowded a place is. The population density for the USA and CIS is very low, showing that neither is very crowded. Japan is very different. It has a large population living in a small area, which means that it has a high population density and is very crowded. In fact, as only 17 per cent of Japan is flat enough to live on, parts of the country have over 1000 people to every square kilometre. Lack of space is one of Japan's biggest problems.

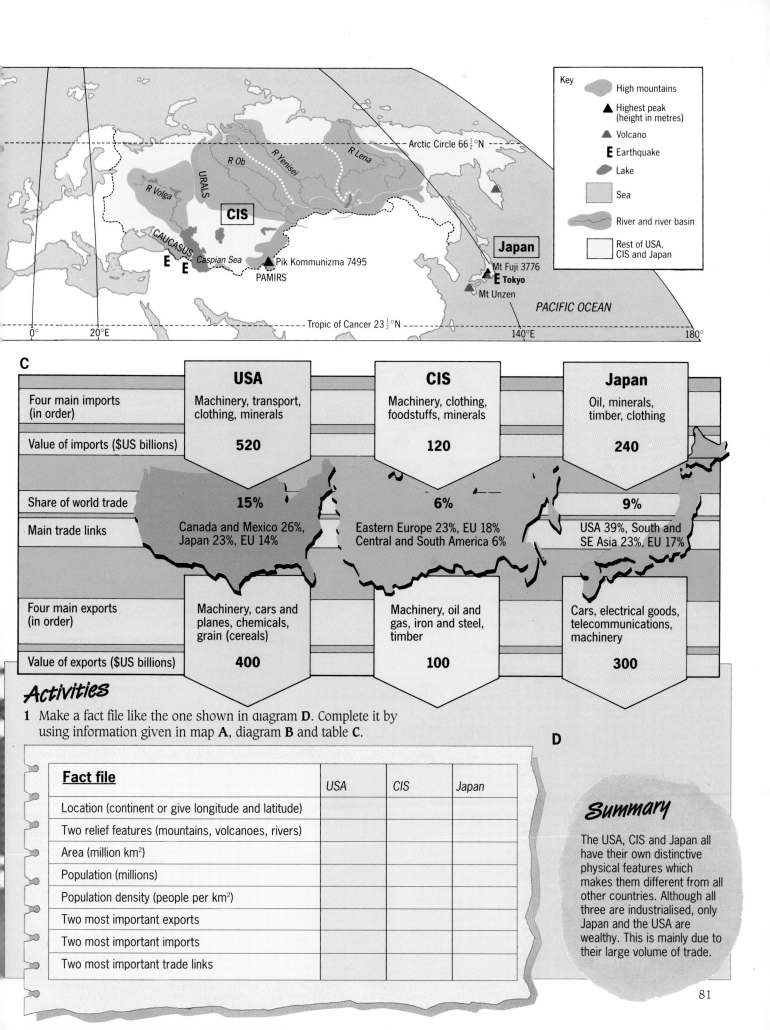

Key
- High mountains
- ▲ Highest peak (height in metres)
- ▲ Volcano
- **E** Earthquake
- Lake
- Sea
- River and river basin
- Rest of USA, CIS and Japan

Arctic Circle 66½°N

R Ob
R Yenisei
R Lena
R Volga
URALS
CIS
CAUCASUS
Caspian Sea
E **E**
Pik Kommunizma 7495
PAMIRS

Japan
Mt Fuji 3776
E Tokyo
Mt Unzen

PACIFIC OCEAN

Tropic of Cancer 23½°N

0°   20°E   140°E   180°

C

	USA	CIS	Japan
Four main imports (in order)	Machinery, transport, clothing, minerals	Machinery, clothing, foodstuffs, minerals	Oil, minerals, timber, clothing
Value of imports ($US billions)	520	120	240
Share of world trade	15%	6%	9%
Main trade links	Canada and Mexico 26%, Japan 23%, EU 14%	Eastern Europe 23%, EU 18% Central and South America 6%	USA 39%, South and SE Asia 23%, EU 17%
Four main exports (in order)	Machinery, cars and planes, chemicals, grain (cereals)	Machinery, oil and gas, iron and steel, timber	Cars, electrical goods, telecommunications, machinery
Value of exports ($US billions)	400	100	300

Activities

1 Make a fact file like the one shown in diagram **D**. Complete it by using information given in map **A**, diagram **B** and table **C**.

D

Fact file	USA	CIS	Japan
Location (continent or give longitude and latitude)			
Two relief features (mountains, volcanoes, rivers)			
Area (million km²)			
Population (millions)			
Population density (people per km²)			
Two most important exports			
Two most important imports			
Two most important trade links			

Summary

The USA, CIS and Japan all have their own distinctive physical features which makes them different from all other countries. Although all three are industrialised, only Japan and the USA are wealthy. This is mainly due to their large volume of trade.

81

▶ *What are the USA's sources of energy?* ◀

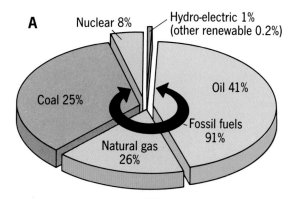

A

Nuclear 8%
Hydro-electric 1% (other renewable 0.2%)
Coal 25%
Oil 41%
Fossil fuels 91%
Natural gas 26%

B

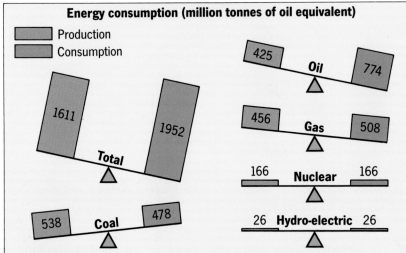

Energy consumption (million tonnes of oil equivalent)

Production
Consumption

1611	1952
	Total
538 **Coal** 478	

425 **Oil** 774	
456 **Gas** 508	
166 **Nuclear** 166	
26 **Hydro-electric** 26	

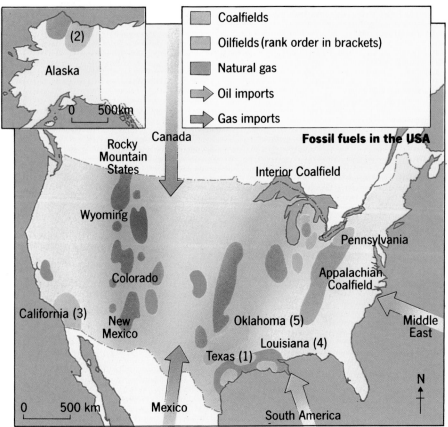

Coalfields
Oilfields (rank order in brackets)
Natural gas
Oil imports
Gas imports

Fossil fuels in the USA

(2)
Alaska
0   500km

Canada
Rocky Mountain States
Interior Coalfield
Wyoming
Pennsylvania
Colorado
Appalachian Coalfield
California (3)
New Mexico
Oklahoma (5)
Middle East
Louisiana (4)
Texas (1)
Mexico
N
South America
0   500 km

C Fossil fuels in the USA

The USA is the world's largest consumer of energy (24.6 per cent of the world's total). In 1990 each American used the same amount of energy as two people living in the EU, ten people living in South America, thirteen people living in Asia and 25 people living in Africa. Fortunately for the USA, it has large and varied energy resources. It also has the capital and technology to develop these resources. In 1990 it was, after the CIS, the world's largest producer of energy (19.4 per cent of the world's total). The USA has used its own energy resources, as well as those of other countries, to develop industry and to reach a high standard of living.

Coal, oil and natural gas provide over 90 per cent of the USA's total energy requirements (graph **A**). A large proportion of these fuels are used to generate electricity. They are fossil fuels which, once burnt, cannot be used again. Most of the remainder of the country's energy requirements are provided by nuclear power. Nuclear power uses uranium which, although not a fossil fuel, is also a non-renewable resource. The USA also has a wide range of renewable resources which include hydro-electric, geothermal, wind, wave and solar power. However, these have only been developed in local areas and, with the exception of hydro-electricity, do not yet make any major contribution to the national power supply.

Non-renewable sources of energy (map C)

Coal, which provided 85 per cent of the USA's energy needs in 1900, still supplied 25 per cent in 1992. The oldest coalmining areas lie in the Appalachian Mountains and to the south of the Great Lakes. Since the 1970s coalfields have been developed near to the Rocky Mountains. Coal in these western states is strip-mined on the surface, by giant excavators. This coal is easier and cheaper to produce and, because it has a lower sulphur content, causes less pollution when burnt. However, this coal has to be transported further to cities, increasing transport costs, and it gives off less heat when burnt. The USA produces sufficient coal for considerable amounts to be exported (graph **B**).

Oil is the USA's most important source of energy. Although the USA is the world's second largest producer of crude oil, it consumes far more than it produces (graph **B**). The gap has to be filled by importing oil from the Middle East (a major reason for America's involvement in the Gulf War) and South America. Although the USA has large oilfields in Texas, Southern California and Alaska, reserves are dwindling. Attempts have been made, since the mid-1970s, to reduce the dependency upon oil in order to conserve the country's remaining reserves and to reduce the cost of oil imports.

Natural gas is an increasingly popular source of energy because it is clean, efficient and easy to move by pipeline. Like oil, the USA consumes more natural gas than it produces and pipelines have been built to import gas from Mexico and Canada. The USA hopes to develop new gasfields off the coast of Alaska and in the Gulf of Mexico.

During the 1970s, nuclear power was regarded as the solution to the USA's energy problem. By 1993 nearly 120 nuclear power stations were operating, mainly along the Atlantic coast and in California. However, since the accident which caused the closure of the Three Mile Island power station in 1979, and following earthquakes in California, opposition to this form of energy has grown considerably.

Renewable sources of energy (map D)

Hydro-electricity is the only form of renewable energy which has been developed on a large scale in the USA. Even so, it is largely limited to the Tennessee, Colorado, Columbia and

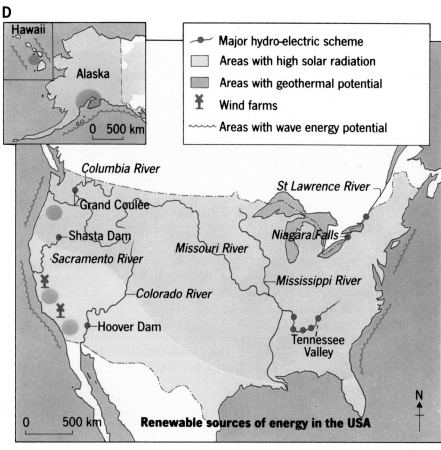

St Lawrence Rivers. Many parts of the USA either have insufficient water or are too distant from urban and industrial centres. Large wind farms are being developed in California and solar power is being used in the sunnier 'south-west' of the country. There appears to be the potential to develop geothermal power in California and wave power off several coasts.

Activities

1 Draw a percentage bar chart to show the types of energy used in the USA.

2 Make a larger copy of table **E**. Complete it by following these instructions.
   a) List the five types of energy used by the USA. Put them in rank order with the highest first.
   b) For each type of energy say if it is renewable, a fossil fuel, or neither.
   c) Name places in the USA where each type of energy can be found.

   d) Name countries (if any) from which the USA has to import some of this type of energy.

3 a) Why does the USA rely upon fossil fuels for most of its energy?
   b) What types of renewable energy are available to the USA?
   c) Why do renewable sources only contribute 1 per cent of the USA's total energy production?

E

Types of energy (rank order)	Renewable energy, fossil fuel or neither	Location in the USA	Countries from which energy is obtained

Summary

The USA is the world's second largest producer and the largest consumer of energy. Over 90 per cent of the country's energy requirements come from fossil fuels. As consumption exceeds production then significant amounts of oil and natural gas have to be imported.

► *Where did early industry locate in the USA?* ◄

Early industries in the USA located in the north-east of the country. The main areas were New England and a region extending from the Great Lakes to the Atlantic coast (map **A**). In 1900 this part of the USA had over 70 per cent of manufacturing jobs and was referred to as the **manufacturing belt**. Industries, such as iron and steel, heavy engineering and car assembly located here for these reasons.

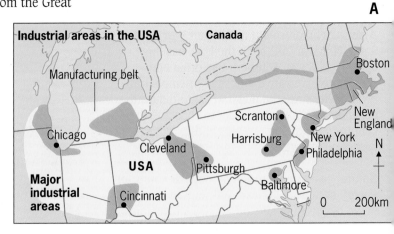

A

Industrial areas in the USA

- Many immigrants from Europe arrived and settled here. They brought with them industrial and business skills.
- The rapid growth in population, due to natural increase and immigration, led to both a large local market and a large supply of labour (workforce). In time the labour supply became increasingly skilled, especially in industries such as car manufacturing.
- The area was rich in raw materials such as coal and iron ore which gave rise to a large iron and steel industry (map **B**).
- Sources of energy were available. Fast-flowing rivers were initially used to turn waterwheels in New England. In the manufacturing belt coal and, later, oil were available locally.
- Transport developed along rivers or on the Great Lakes. The Atlantic coast faced Europe with which the region established trade links. Water transport has always been the cheapest method of moving bulky goods.
- The wealth generated by selling goods overseas enabled the region to invest in new technology and to produce a wider range of products at competitive prices.

Over time the ideal site for the location of steelworks has changed (map **B**).

B The development of the iron and steel industry

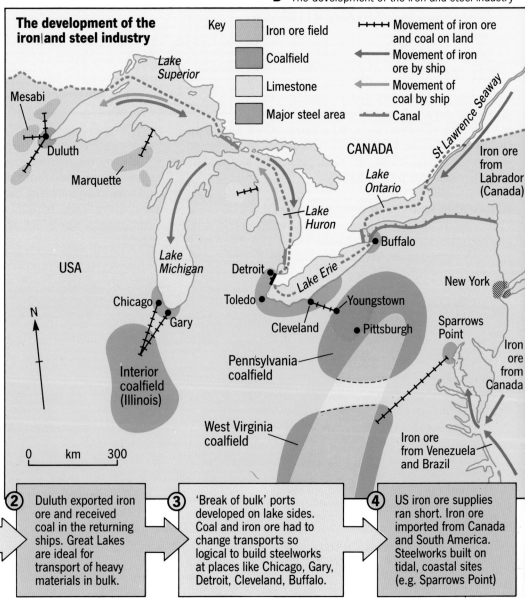

① The first iron and steel works were located on coal fields. Rivers and lakes were used to transport iron ore and coal. Pittsburgh, Youngstown

② Duluth exported iron ore and received coal in the returning ships. Great Lakes are ideal for transport of heavy materials in bulk.

③ 'Break of bulk' ports developed on lake sides. Coal and iron ore had to change transports so logical to build steelworks at places like Chicago, Gary, Detroit, Cleveland, Buffalo.

④ US iron ore supplies ran short. Iron ore imported from Canada and South America. Steelworks built on tidal, coastal sites (e.g. Sparrows Point)

Detroit – the centre for car production

Detroit was near to local steelworks and the many smaller factories which produced the component parts needed for car assembly. It also had easy access to energy supplies. Nearby was a large labour force, both skilled and unskilled. In time the car industry became increasingly mechanised, although this meant repetitive work. Car companies expected high productivity and standards for the wages paid. Detroit was centrally placed for the assembly of car parts and the sale of vehicles. It was also in a good position to export surplus cars to overseas markets. There was plenty of space on which to build the large car factories and room for later expansion (photo **D**). Even so, Detroit became the centre for cars partly due to chance, because Henry Ford, the founder of the Ford Motor Company, just happened to live there.

Since the 1970s, many of the major industries in the manufacturing belt have declined. This has partly been due to a fall in demand for such products as iron and steel, heavy engineering and motor vehicles and partly because modern factories have been located in places with a more attractive environment and climate (the sunbelt - page 86). As factories have closed and people have migrated away from the region, the manufacturing belt has been renamed the **rustbelt**. In 1990 less than 35 per cent of manufacturing jobs were found in this region.

C Steelworks at Baltimore – coastal location

D
General Motors Hamtramck Assembly Plant, Detroit

Activities

1 a) Where was the so-called 'manufacturing belt' in the USA?
   b) Draw a star diagram to show six advantages for early industry locating in the manufacturing belt.
   c) How important were sources of energy in the growth of industry in the manufacturing belt?

   Pittsburgh → Duluth → Cleveland → Sparrows Point **E**

2 a) The ideal location for iron and steel works in the manufacturing belt have changed over a period of time. Explain why each of the places named in diagram **E** became important for the production of iron and steel.
   b) What advantages did Detroit have which enabled it to become the world's leading producer of cars?

Summary

Sources of energy were only one reason why industries such as iron and steel, heavy engineering and car assembly became important in the manufacturing belt of the USA.

► *Why has modern industry changed location in the USA?* ◄

Many modern industries are said to be **footloose**. The term footloose means that, unlike older industries, firms have a relatively free choice of where to locate and are not tied to being near to raw materials. As many of these newer industries provide services for people they are best located near to large markets where people are likely to buy, or use, the products. Usually both the component parts and the finished product are light in weight and so they can easily be transported by road and air. Americans, with their high standard of living, increasingly want to live and work in a more pleasant environment. A pleasant environment includes plenty of open space, attractive scenery, leisure amenities, modern services and an agreeable climate. The result has been that, since the 1970s, firms and people have been moving away from the manufacturing/rust belt to the **sunbelt** (table **A**).

The term sunbelt was originally applied to five states in the south-west of the USA where population and economic growth rates were far in excess of the national averages

A

Six fastest growing states 1980-90		Six slowest growing states 1980-90	
(percentage growth of population)			
Nevada	50.1	West Virginia	-8.0
Alaska	36.9	Iowa	-4.7
Arizona	34.8	North Dakota	-2.1
Florida	32.7	Illinois	0
California	25.7	Pennsylvania	0.1
Texas	20.5	Michigan	0.4

(map **B**). The rapid growth of high-technology (sunrise) industries and their good job opportunities attracted many younger people from the depressed industrial (sunset) areas of the north and east. The term sunbelt is now often applied more widely to include all states in the south and south-east of the country.

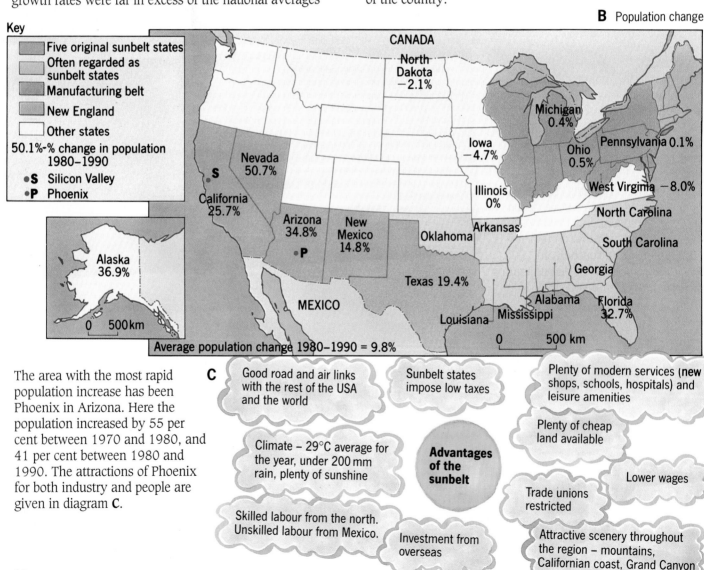

B Population change

Key
- Five original sunbelt states
- Often regarded as sunbelt states
- Manufacturing belt
- New England
- Other states
- 50.1%-% change in population 1980–1990
- **S** Silicon Valley
- **P** Phoenix

Average population change 1980–1990 = 9.8%

The area with the most rapid population increase has been Phoenix in Arizona. Here the population increased by 55 per cent between 1970 and 1980, and 41 per cent between 1980 and 1990. The attractions of Phoenix for both industry and people are given in diagram **C**.

C

Good road and air links with the rest of the USA and the world

Sunbelt states impose low taxes

Plenty of modern services (**new** shops, schools, hospitals) and leisure amenities

Climate – 29°C average for the year, under 200 mm rain, plenty of sunshine

Advantages of the sunbelt

Plenty of cheap land available

Lower wages

Trade unions restricted

Skilled labour from the north. Unskilled labour from Mexico.

Investment from overseas

Attractive scenery throughout the region – mountains, Californian coast, Grand Canyon

The greatest concentration of high-technology industry in the USA is Silicon Valley to the south of San Francisco in California (diagram **D** and photo **E**). The area produces over 25 per cent of America's micro-electronics, computers, and scientific instruments. Like elsewhere in California, Silicon Valley has many firms connected with the aerospace and defence industries.

D

Why does high-technology industry locate in Silicon Valley?

- Near to major road systems (internal transport) and airports (international trade).
- Plenty of space for development and future expansion.
- Near to large cities (markets and a skilled workforce) yet far enough away for land values to be lower than in urban areas.
- Near to universities which include some of the most advanced scientific and technological centres in the world.
- Clean and quiet industries do not pollute an attractive environment and a pleasant climate.

Two factors could slow down the movement of people and industry to the sunbelt. The first is the problem of water supply. Many parts of the region have a desert climate with little, or unreliable, rainfall. Already many places rely upon water being piped vast distances. The second is the uncertain future of the aerospace (high costs) and defence (reduced military spending) industries.

E

Silicon Valley

Activities

1 a) Make a larger copy of map **F**.
   b) Name the original five sunbelt states (labelled **A** to **E**).
   c) Name, with the help of an atlas, the six cities (numbered **1** to **6**).
   d) Name the two sea areas (labelled **X** and **Y**).

2 You are the managing director of a small, but expanding, computer firm in Pennsylvania. Make a list of reasons why you decide
   a) not to expand your factory in Pennsylvania,
   b) to have a new factory built in one of the sunbelt states.

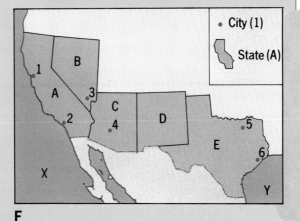

F

Summary

Many firms and people have left the old manufacturing belt of the USA and moved south-westwards into the sunbelt. Firms have moved as new footloose high-technology industry is no longer tied to raw materials. People have moved as they prefer to live and work in a more pleasant environment.

▶ *How has industry affected the environment of the USA?* ◀

As the USA developed its industries it gave little thought as to how this would affect the environment. By the 1970s water supplies and the air had become severely polluted. This began to cause serious health problems for people and was posing a threat to the existence of wildlife. The worst affected areas were around the Great Lakes and in the manufacturing belt. These places had high population densities, many large industries, thermal power stations and an increasing number of cars.

Water pollution

Diagram **A** includes an extract describing conditions around the southern shores of Lake Erie twenty years ago. It was estimated that the pollution was caused by over 1000 chemicals being released directly into, or finding their way to, the Great Lakes. These came from steel works (page 84), the petroleum industry, paper mills and car assembly plants. Since then attempts have been made to clean up the Great Lakes and other polluted rivers (map **B**). Despite big improvements, the pollution of earlier years cannot be cleaned up overnight. Indeed recent investigations have shown that major breeding problems exist, with a decline in the fertility of fish, mammals, reptiles and birds in the Great Lakes area. The number of alligators in Florida has also declined. It is believed that certain industrial chemicals, together with pesticides, are turning male alligators into females. As water is sometimes taken from rivers and treated before its domestic use, then this may also explain the decrease in human fertility. Map **B** also shows the worst polluted sea areas which surround the USA.

A

In the Great Lakes region of North America, various pollutants have made Lake Erie a 'dead lake'.

One of the Nation's most polluted streams, Ohio's Cuyahoga became so covered with oil and debris that in July 1969 the river caught fire in Cleveland's factory area, damaging two railway bridges. Along this six-mile stretch, before emptying into Lake Eris, the river receives the wastes of steel mills, chemical and meat-rendering plants, and other industries. Just upstream, Cleveland and Akron discharge inadequately treated sewage. And from hinterland farms drain phosphate- and nitrate- rich fertilizers and poisonous pesticides.

The Cuyahoga flows into Lake Erie, mixing with effluent from the Detroit Rover. The flow, rich in nutrients, stimulates growth of algae. As the overfertilized algae die and decompose, oxygen essential to fish life is depleted.

Lake Erie is said to be 'too thick to drink, too thin to plough'.

B

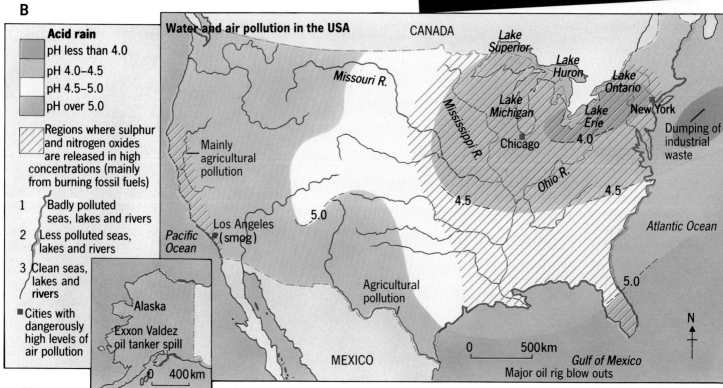

Water and air pollution in the USA

Acid rain
- pH less than 4.0
- pH 4.0–4.5
- pH 4.5–5.0
- pH over 5.0

Regions where sulphur and nitrogen oxides are released in high concentrations (mainly from burning fossil fuels)

1 Badly polluted seas, lakes and rivers
2 Less polluted seas, lakes and rivers
3 Clean seas, lakes and rivers
■ Cities with dangerously high levels of air pollution

Alaska
Exxon Valdez oil tanker spill
0   400 km

Mainly agricultural pollution

Los Angeles (smog)

Pacific Ocean

Agricultural pollution

MEXICO

CANADA
Lake Superior
Lake Huron
Lake Ontario
Missouri R.
Lake Michigan
Lake Erie
New York
Chicago — 4.0
Mississippi R.
Ohio R.
4.5
4.5
5.0
5.0

Dumping of industrial waste

Atlantic Ocean

0   500km

Gulf of Mexico
Major oil rig blow outs

N

Air pollution

The burning of fossil fuels in factories, thermal power stations and by motor vehicles releases sulphur dioxide and nitrogen oxide (photo **C**, page 85). It is these pollutants which cause acid rain (page 30). Acid rain destroys forests, kills fish and plant life in lakes, increases acidity in soils and wears away buildings. Most of the pollutants which contribute to acid rain in North America are released in the manufacturing belt of the USA. However, due to the prevailing westerly winds, the greatest effects are felt by places lying to the east (map **B**).

Smog is a second type of air pollution. It is a thick fog which contains pollutants released from the burning of fossil fuels in factories and thermal power stations and from fumes released by car exhausts. In Los Angeles smog can be expected on up to 300 days in a year. Fog forms when warm air from the land meets cold air from the Californian Current (page 25). Fog is worst when the wind blows from the sea in summer (diagram **C** and photo **D**). As the sea is cooler than the land at this time of year, the wind blowing from it will also be cold (page 9). The cold air undercuts the warmer air to give a **temperature inversion**. Normally the temperature of the air decreases with height (page 9), but during a time of temperature inversion a layer of warm air lies on top of the cold air. Smog forms because smoke and exhaust fumes cannot rise above the inversion and so become trapped. Smog causes breathing difficulties and makes eyes sting. It can be fatal to people with asthma, bronchitis and other severe breathing problems.

C Formation of smog in Los Angeles

'Normal' conditions

Temperatures decrease with height

Warm air containing smoke and car fumes can rise and escape

Factories, power stations, eight-lane highways

Coast range

Los Angeles confined between mountains and the sea

Land is warm. Air over land is warmed and rises.

Pacific Ocean

Temperature inversion

Warmer, cleaner air

Above here temperatures decrease with height

Inversion layer

Cold air undercuts warm air

Smog

Coast range

Cold/cool wind from the sea

Cold California current (Page 25)

Smoke and car fumes trapped within cold air layer. Cannot rise and escape.

Pacific Ocean

D
Smog in Los Angeles

Activities

1 a) What were the main causes and effects of pollution in Lake Erie twenty years ago?
   b) What is the latest concern believed to be caused by industrial chemicals being released into lakes and water supplies?

2 a) Which part of the USA is the major contributor to acid rain?
   b) Why are the worst effects of acid rain not always experienced in this part of the USA?
   c) What is smog?
   d) What are the causes and effects of smog in Los Angeles?

Summary

The rapid growth of industry caused serious water and air pollution in parts of the USA. The task of cleaning up the environment, which takes a long time and costs a lot of money, is difficult so long as fossil fuels are burnt and the number of cars increase.

►Why are there variations in economic prosperity in the USA? ◄

Economic growth is rarely evenly distributed. Growth becomes concentrated in a few favoured locations leaving other places relatively poor and underdeveloped in comparison. This can be seen at different levels - in a city, in a region, in a country and between countries.

Core-periphery model

The most prosperous and developed part of a country is called the **core**. The core is likely to contain the capital city, the chief port and the major industrial areas (diagram **A (a)**). As the core continues to grow and to develop it will attract other industries and services such as banking, insurance and government offices. As levels of capital and technology increase, the region will be able to afford schools, hospitals, shopping centres, a modern transport system and better quality housing. These 'pull' factors encourage people to migrate from the surrounding rural areas. Often the level of wealth and development decreases with distance from the core so that the poorest areas are towards the **periphery** of the country (diagram **A (a)**). In the periphery jobs will be few in number, poorly paid, relatively unskilled and mainly in the primary sector. Services and government investment are usually limited. These 'push' factors force many people to migrate out of the area.

As a country develops economically, industry and wealth begin to spread out. Initially a second core region will develop (diagram **A (b)**), followed by several secondary core regions (diagram **A (c)**). This results in a decline in the dominance of the original core. Although wealth will now be more evenly spread around the country, there will still be periphery areas which are less well off.

A

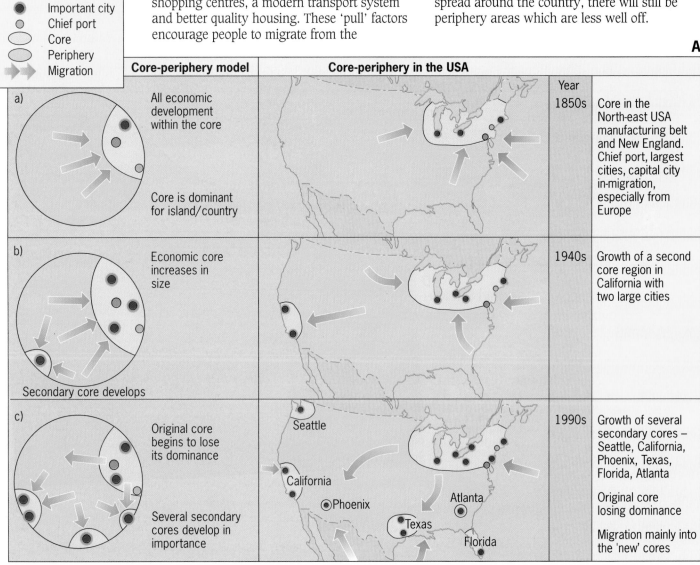

Key
- Capital city
- Important city
- Chief port
- Core
- Periphery
- Migration

Core-periphery model

a) All economic development within the core

Core is dominant for island/country

b) Economic core increases in size

Secondary core develops

c) Original core begins to lose its dominance

Several secondary cores develop in importance

Core-periphery in the USA

Seattle
California
Phoenix
Texas
Atlanta
Florida

Year	
1850s	Core in the North-east USA manufacturing belt and New England. Chief port, largest cities, capital city in-migration, especially from Europe
1940s	Growth of a second core region in California with two large cities
1990s	Growth of several secondary cores – Seattle, California, Phoenix, Texas, Florida, Atlanta. Original core losing dominance. Migration mainly into the 'new' cores

Variations in wealth and development in American cities

You may have a perception that, if you were a wealthy American, you would probably live somewhere like Miami (Florida) or Los Angeles (California). Perhaps your ideal 'home' is a mansion next to the film stars who live in Malibu (hoping it will not be destroyed by forest fires or landslides!). It is possible, however, that you have an alternative perception. You may think of Miami as a place where foreign tourists are mugged and sometimes killed, while Los Angeles is a city where severe riots take place.

Los Angeles, like many other large American cities, has two faces (diagram **B**). One face shows an economic development which has resulted in an exceptionally high standard of living (photo **C**). The other face shows extreme poverty with severe social, economic and environmental problems (photo **E**). The gap, in wealth, between the two faces is extremely wide. The distance, in kilometres, between them is very small (map **D**).

B

Well off areas (shaded green on map)

Ninety per cent of people are white. The average annual income is over $50 000 per family. Many houses are large with swimming pools and spacious gardens. Many families employ servants. There is easy access to the beach and services such as shops, schools and hospitals. Most families have two or more cars.

Least well off areas (shaded orange on map)

Less than 15 per cent of the people are white. In some districts 70 per cent are black and in others 70 per cent are Hispanic (mainly from Mexico). The average annual family income is $10 000. Housing is poor and overcrowded. People live in run-down tenements which lack basic amenities. An increasing number are homeless and sleep on the streets. Unemployment is high (50 per cent among black people). There are high rates of crime (gang warfare, drug dealing) and racial tension. There is also a high rate of migration of Hispanics from Mexico, many of whom enter the country illegally.

C

D

To San Francisco

Beverly Hills — Holly-wood

Malibu

State highways

To San Diego and Mexico

Long Beach

Harbour

0   20 km

N

Key
D   Downtown (CBD)
Los Angeles
Most wealthy areas
Least wealthy areas

E

Activities

1 Explain, with the help of a simple diagram, the meaning of the terms 'core' and 'periphery'.

2 a) Copy and complete the table below to show how the core region in the USA shows the characteristics of the model.
   b) Which was the second core region to develop in the USA?
   c) How does the core-periphery model help to explain the differences in the economic development of the USA in the 1990s?

3 Describe the differences in wealth and development in Los Angeles under the following headings.
   • Racial groups
   • Family income
   • Housing
   • Employment
   • Social/living conditions.

Summary

Wealth and economic development are never evenly spread out. The core-periphery model can be used to try to explain the causes and consequences of uneven development in either a country or a city.

Location	Two industrial regions	Capital city	Chief port	Three other major cities	Immigration from

9 Brazil, a developing country
► How have the Brazilian Amerindians adapted to the environment? ◄

The tropical rainforest of Brazil is home to numerous Amerindian tribes. However, their numbers have declined rapidly since the arrival of the first Europeans and recent so-called attempts to 'develop' the region. Those Amerindians who remain still

* have a daily life-style which hardly alters from year to year;
* live in harmony with their environment. Their housing, clothing, diet, transport and way of life are affected by the equatorial climate (page 18), the tropical rainforest (page 32), and the rivers of the Amazon drainage basin.

The Tukano
Several small tribes are grouped together to form the larger Tukano tribe. The Tukano tribe live in an isolated part of north-west Brazil, near to the border with Colombia. It is this isolation from the outside world which has enabled the Tukano to preserve their way of life and their culture. Although small in stature (men are usually less than 170 cms tall and women 150 cms), the Tukano are very strong and are not affected by the high humidity. Families rarely have more than two or three living children. The men are usually named after forest birds, the women after forest plants and flowers.

Houses
The Tukano live in large communal houses called malocas (photo **A**). Each maloca is built in a clearing in the forest, may be many kilometres from the next maloca, and can only be reached by river (diagram **B**). The Tukano's maloca has a rectangular shape and often measures over 40 metres in length, 20 metres in width and 12 metres in height. It is built from local forest materials. The main wooden supports, made from trunks of large hardwood trees, are bound together by lianas (page 32). Large palm leaves, and sometimes flattened tree bark, are woven to form a thatch for the roof and walls. The door for the men is at the front and the door for the women is at the rear (diagram **C**).

Inside, the central front area is used by the men and is the focal point for ritual life, political meetings and entertaining visitors. The area surrounding the four central posts is used for dancing.

The rear central part of the maloca is where the women spend most of their days, usually in preparing cassava (page 94). Palm leaves are also used for screens which divide the sides at the rear of the house into a series of compartments, one for each family. Hammocks are strung across each compartment. Weapons for hunting and tools for clearing the forest lie against the walls, while ripening fruit and freshly caught fish hang from the roof. The men tend to store their few possessions in wooden boxes while the women keep theirs in baskets.

A A Tukano maloca

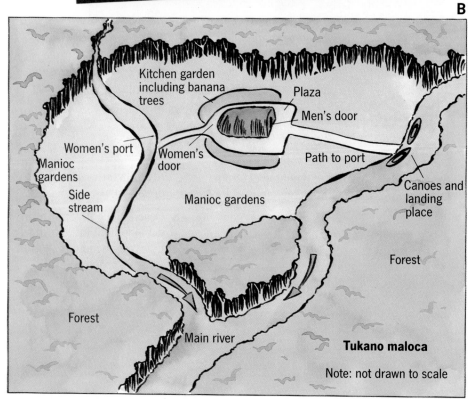

B

Kitchen garden including banana trees

Plaza

Men's door

Women's port

Women's door

Path to port

Manioc gardens

Side stream

Manioc gardens

Canoes and landing place

Forest

Forest

Main river

Tukano maloca

Note: not drawn to scale

C The interior of a Tukano maloca

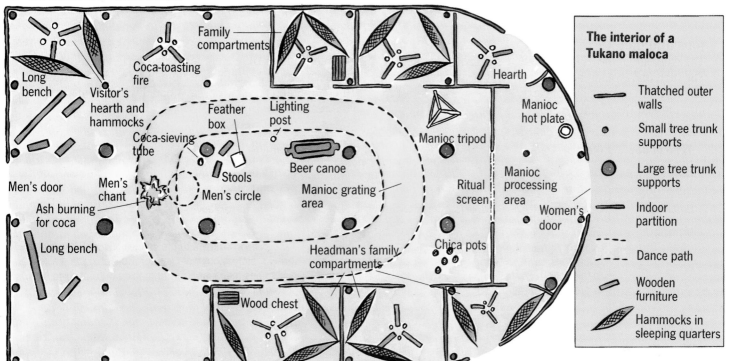

The interior of a Tukano maloca

▬	Thatched outer walls
○	Small tree trunk supports
⬤	Large tree trunk supports
▬	Indoor partition
- - -	Dance path
▱	Wooden furniture
◣	Hammocks in sleeping quarters

Labels on diagram: Family compartments, Coca-toasting fire, Long bench, Visitor's hearth and hammocks, Feather box, Lighting post, Hearth, Manioc hot plate, Manioc tripod, Coca-sieving tube, Beer canoe, Manioc processing area, Men's door, Men's chant, Stools, Men's circle, Manioc grating area, Ritual screen, Women's door, Ash burning for coca, Long bench, Headman's family compartments, Chica pots, Wood chest

Dress

As the Tukano live in a hot, wet climate traditional clothing was a loincloth. Women and girls wear their hair long while men and boys have theirs cut short. Both sexes paint their faces with a red powder obtained by boiling the leaves of a vine. Women accentuate their hair and jaw lines with a black dye obtained from another plant. At dances, further dyes are applied and ornaments are added. The most elaborate item of clothing is the head-dress which often incorporates macaw, egret and parrot feathers (photo **D**).

D Tukano Indian wearing a ceremonial head-dress

Activities

1 a) Where do the Tukano tribe live?
  b) How have they managed to preserve their traditional life-style?

2 a) What is a maloca?
  b) Draw a sketch of a maloca. Add labels to show its size and the materials used to build it.
  c) Either draw a plan or write a short account to describe the inside of a maloca.

Summary The climate and vegetation of the Amazon rainforest affects the housing of the people who live there.

How has the environment affected the Amerindians' daily life?

Jobs and diet

The daily life of the Tukano Indians is described in table **A**. The men and women have different but clearly defined roles. The men are responsible for clearing new areas of forest for farming and they hunt for food. The women do all the

farming (photo **B**), except for the collection of coca and tobacco leaves. Most of their time, however, is spent preparing and cooking cassava bread which is made from the manioc plant (photo **D**).

A

Time of day	Men		Women
Early morning	Wash in river		Up before dawn. Light fires since it is quite cool. Collect water from river.
Breakfast	Cassava bread, juice, leftovers from previous night. Men and women eat separately.		
Morning	*Either:* (a) Clear new area of forest using machetes and axes to fell trees.Trees burned to produce fertiliser.	(b) Hunting expedition for fish or meat (tapir, monkey, parrot). Use spears, bows and arrows and blowpipes.	Take manioc baskets to the chagras (fields). Weed crops (grow rapidly in hot wet climate). Collect some maize, pineapples, bananas. Uproot manioc (a plant used to prepare cassava). Plant/collect yams, beans and peppers. Plant manioc in ash.
Lunch	Cassava bread (eaten at all meals), fresh fruit (bananas, pineapples)		
Afternoon	(a) Short rest in heat of the day. Collect coca and tobacco leaves (the only male farming job done once the land is cleared). Make baskets and strings of beads, smoke.	(b) May still be on hunting expedition, especially if looking for meat`	Wash freshly collected manioc, dirty pots and children in river. Spend most of afternoon preparing cassava bread – manioc is grated, the resultant pulp is sieved through baskets, water is added and then the pulp is sqeezed through a cassava press to separate the tapioca starch from a poisonous juice (used by the men in hunting). The starch is flattened and cooked to make cassava bread. Young girls make pots.
Evening meal	Cooked fish and/or meat, freshly cooked vegetables and cassava bread and juice		
Evening	Drink chicha (home-made beer) and chew coca leaves (gives hallucinations), play musical instruments (panpipes, drums). Many rituals and festivals with drinking and dancing		Supervise younger children. Time spent separate from the men until evening or when allowed to join in specific festivals

B (*Left*) An area of forest cleared for farming by the Tukano, known as a chagra

C (*Right*) Men weaving baskets for sieving manioc

Transport

Travel by the Tukano is almost entirely on water. Although they travel on foot through the rainforest on hunting expeditions, dug-out canoes are used to go further afield, either to fish or to trade with other tribes. Like most other forest tribes, the Tukano have evolved their own methods of making canoes. A large tree is felled. A seven metre section is cut, its bark removed and the log is left for several weeks to dry. Using an azador, a curved hoe-like blade, the outside of the log is shaped and the centre is cut out (photo **E**), making sure that the sides are not cut too thin. The final process is to gently burn the sides.

Why is the traditional Amerindian way of life changing?

The Tukano, like most other Amerindian tribes, are **shifting cultivators**. They clear small areas of forest for their malocas and chagras. As the cleared area no longer has a protective tree cover, then humus in the soil cannot be replaced and the heavy rainfall is not intercepted by leaves and branches. Within four or five years nutrients in the soil will have been washed away (leached) and the land will have become infertile. The forest Indians overcame this problem by moving their home every few years. Recently, large areas of rainforest have been cleared for commercial reasons (pages 38 to 39). These clearances, known as deforestation, have had a dramatic effect upon the lives of people, wildlife and the environment of the rainforest (pages 40 to 43). The number of Indians has declined rapidly, their freedom to move around the forest has been reduced, and their daily way of life (culture) has been altered.

D Women preparing cassava bread from the sieved manioc

E A Tukano Indian and canoe

Activities

1 a) Describe the daily life of a Tukano man and a Tukano women.
   b) How is daily life of the Tukano affected by
   i)   the landscape,
   ii) the weather,
   iii) wealth?
   c) Why is transport on water so important in the lives of the Tukano?

2 a) Briefly describe the traditional way of life of the Tukano.
   b) Why is it claimed that this 'traditional way of life was in harmony with the environment'?

Summary The daily life of people living in the Amazon rainforest was related to, and was affected by, the environment and location of the region. This traditional way of life is being altered by recent changes in human activity.

▶ *What are the main physical features of Brazil?* ◀

We have already seen that it is often physical factors which determine

- **population distribution** – i.e. where people live;
- **population density** – i.e. why some places are crowded while others have few people living there.

Physical factors include climate, natural vegetation, relief, soils and natural resources (raw materials). These two pages describe the physical features of Brazil. Pages 98 and 99 show how these features have influenced the distribution of population in that country.

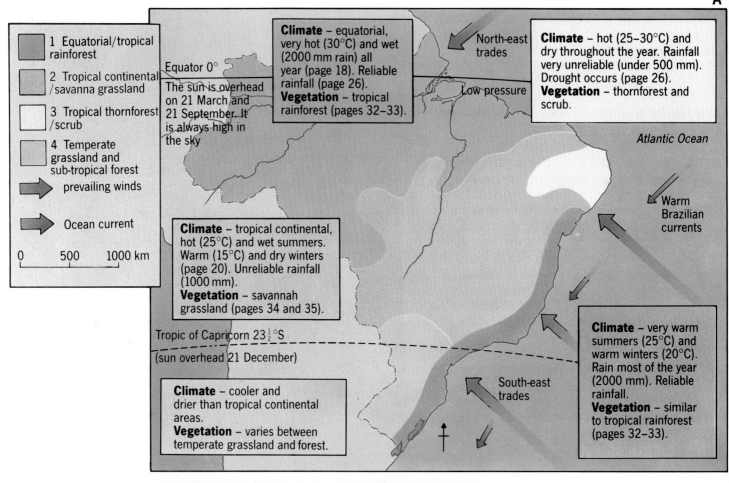

A

Key:

1 Equatorial/tropical rainforest

2 Tropical continental /savanna grassland

3 Tropical thornforest /scrub

4 Temperate grassland and sub-tropical forest

→ prevailing winds

→ Ocean current

0   500   1000 km

Equator 0°

The sun is overhead on 21 March and 21 September. It is always high in the sky

Climate – equatorial, very hot (30°C) and wet (2000 mm rain) all year (page 18). Reliable rainfall (page 26).
Vegetation – tropical rainforest (pages 32–33).

North-east trades

Low pressure

Climate – hot (25–30°C) and dry throughout the year. Rainfall very unreliable (under 500 mm). Drought occurs (page 26).
Vegetation – thornforest and scrub.

Atlantic Ocean

Warm Brazilian currents

Climate – tropical continental, hot (25°C) and wet summers. Warm (15°C) and dry winters (page 20). Unreliable rainfall (1000 mm).
Vegetation – savannah grassland (pages 34 and 35).

Tropic of Capricorn 23½°S

(sun overhead 21 December)

Climate – cooler and drier than tropical continental areas.
Vegetation – varies between temperate grassland and forest.

South-east trades

Climate – very warm summers (25°C) and warm winters (20°C). Rain most of the year (2000 mm). Reliable rainfall.
Vegetation – similar to tropical rainforest (pages 32–33).

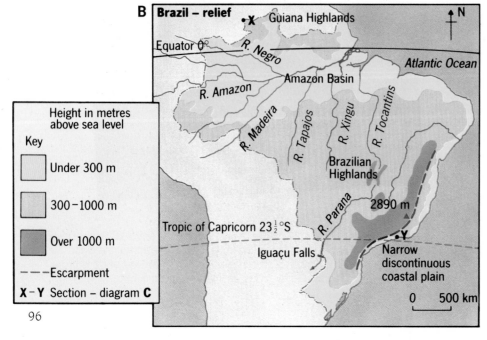

B **Brazil – relief**

• **X** Guiana Highlands

Equator 0°

R. Negro

Amazon Basin

R. Amazon

R. Madeira

R. Tapajos

R. Xingu

R. Tocantins

Atlantic Ocean

Brazilian Highlands

R. Parana

2890 m

Tropic of Capricorn 23½°S

Iguaçu Falls

Narrow discontinuous coastal plain

N

Key:

Height in metres above sea level

Under 300 m

300–1000 m

Over 1000 m

- - - Escarpment

X – Y Section – diagram **C**

0   500 km

Map **A** briefly describes the major differences in the climate and vegetation of Brazil. Most of the country experiences either an equatorial climate (page 18) with tropical rainforest vegetation (pages 32-33) or a tropical continental climate (page 20) with savanna grassland vegetation (pages 34-35). Remember that climate is related to latitude and distance from the sea (page 8); prevailing winds and relief (page 9); ocean currents (page 24); and to different types of rainfall (pages 10 and 11) and its reliability (page 26).

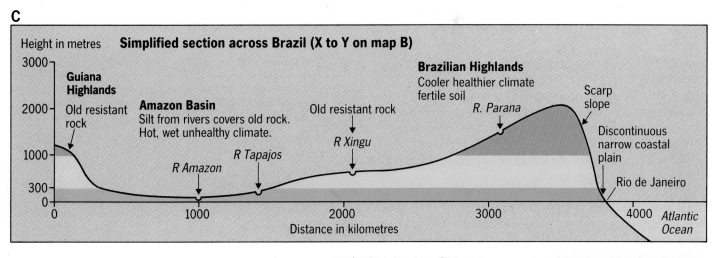

C

Height in metres **Simplified section across Brazil (X to Y on map B)**

Guiana Highlands
Old resistant rock

Amazon Basin
Silt from rivers covers old rock. Hot, wet unhealthy climate.

Old resistant rock

R Xingu

R Tapajos

R Amazon

Brazilian Highlands
Cooler healthier climate fertile soil

R. Parana

Scarp slope

Discontinuous narrow coastal plain

Rio de Janeiro

Atlantic Ocean

Distance in kilometres

Map **B** and diagram **C** have both been simplified. Map **B** shows the relief of Brazil (highland and main rivers). Diagram **C** is a cross-section taken from the north-west of the country to the south-east. Remember that while most people living in Britain usually choose to live in flat, low-lying areas, in the tropics people often prefer to live in more highland areas where the climate is both cooler and more healthy.

People, in which ever country they live, are attracted to places which have considerable natural resources. Natural resources include fertile soils, mineral deposits and energy supplies. Map **D** shows the location of the more important natural resources in Brazil. The first natural resources to be utilised in Brazil were in the south-east. It is only during the last two decades that many more mineral deposits have been discovered and, like several of the energy supplies, developed. Most of this recent development has occurred in the Amazon rainforest (page 41).

Brazil – natural resources

Recent exploitation of gold and silver

R. Amazon

Hydro-electric (HEP) potential

Pitinga – tin

Amapa – manganese
Trombetas – bauxite
Tucurui HEP station

Carajas – iron ore and, nearby, gold

Lead

Gold

Salvador
Small oilfield

Minas Gerais (oldest mining area) – iron ore, manganese, gold, precious stones including diamonds

Itaipo HEP station

Copper
Coal

Atlantic Ocean

Mineral	World rank	% total
Tin	1	22
Iron ore	2	11
Bauxite	4	7.5
Manganese	6	7.7
Gold	7	4.4
(1990)		

D

Key
Forest products
Energy
Minerals
Rich soils

Activities

1 Map **E** has been simplified to show four different regions in Brazil.
   a) Make a copy of table **F** and complete it by using the information given on these two pages.
   b) Which of the regions do you consider to have the
      i) most physical advantages?
      ii) least physical advantages?
   Give reasons for your answer.

E

F

Region	Map number	Climate	Vegetation	Relief and drainage	Soils	Water supply	Energy	Minerals
Amazon Basin								
Brazilian Highlands								
North-east Brazil								
East Coast								

Summary

The distribution of population within a region, country or continent is often influenced by physical factors which include climate, vegetation, relief, soils and natural resources.

▶ *How is Brazil's population distributed?* ◀

Brazil's population, like that of every other country, is not evenly spread out. Some parts of the country are very crowded while others have relatively few people living there. This uneven distribution of population is mainly a result of:

- migration – the movement of people into and within the country.
- physical conditions – the influence of climate, relief and raw materials (pages 96-7).

The movement of people into Brazil

The present inhabitants of Brazil are descended from four main groups of people who arrived in the country from different directions (map **A**). The Amerindians of the Amazon basin are believed to have originated in eastern Asia and migrated to America along with the Incas (Andes), Aztecs (Mexico) and the North American Indians. The Portuguese, who ruled Brazil for several centuries, were the first Europeans to arrive. Most of the Portuguese were young men, many of whom married black slaves brought from Africa. The present population is derived from several ethnic groups and mixed marriages. Brazil is proud of its racial harmony and relative lack of discrimination and prejudice.

Differences in physical conditions

Brazil is the fifth largest country, by area, in the world. It is bigger than the whole of Europe (excluding the CIS). In a country of this size there is a wide range of physical conditions. Sometimes these conditions are positive and attract people to an area. Sometimes they are negative and discourage settlement. Map **B** shows a simple distribution

A

Amerindians from Eastern Asia –about 1200 years ago
1492–estimated 6 million
1992–estimated 0.2 million

After 1500, many Portuguese settled along the north-east coast, and later along the south-east coast

Most settled in the rainforests of the Amazon Basin

Equator

1600-1850 African slaves mainly coasta areas

Central areas received few immigrants

N

0   500km

Early 20th century – many Japanese settled in São Paulo

After 1850 an increasi number of Italians, Spaniards and German settled in the south-eas often in the Brazilian Highlands

pattern in Brazil. The most densely populated areas are found in the south-east of the country. Population decreases rapidly towards the north and west where the density is sparse.

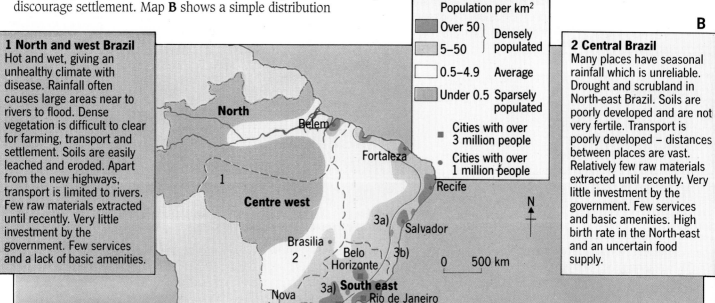

Population per km²

- Over 50 } Densely populated
- 5–50 } populated
- 0.5–4.9 Average
- Under 0.5 Sparsely populated
- ■ Cities with over 3 million people
- • Cities with over 1 million people

B

1 North and west Brazil
Hot and wet, giving an unhealthy climate with disease. Rainfall often causes large areas near to rivers to flood. Dense vegetation is difficult to clear for farming, transport and settlement. Soils are easily leached and eroded. Apart from the new highways, transport is limited to rivers. Few raw materials extracted until recently. Very little investment by the government. Few services and a lack of basic amenities.

2 Central Brazil
Many places have seasonal rainfall which is unreliable. Drought and scrubland in North-east Brazil. Soils are poorly developed and are not very fertile. Transport is poorly developed – distances between places are vast. Relatively few raw materials extracted until recently. Very little investment by the government. Few services and basic amenities. High birth rate in the North-east and an uncertain food supply.

3a South-east Brazil
Highlands are cooler and more healthy than lowland areas. Rainfall is usually reliable. Rich terra rossa soils are ideal for growing coffee. Many minerals – iron ore, gold, precious stones. Transport networks are well-developed. Much government investment. Many services and amenities. Major industrial areas around São Paulo and Belo Horizonte.

3b Coastal areas of Brazil
Rainfall throughout the year gives a reliable water supply. Several flat coastal plains with silt deposited by rivers. Natural harbours developed as ports to receive immigrants and for trade. Much government investment. Many services and amenities. Port industries (Rio de Janeiro) and tourism (Rio and Salvador, the Old Portuguese capital).

Recent movements of population

In Brazil, as in all economically developing countries, there has been a rapid movement of people from the countryside to the towns and cities (diagram **C**). The result of this rural-to-urban migration has been the increase in urbanisation (graph **E**) and the associated problems of urban growth. There have been smaller movements away from the south-east due to:

- the Brazilian government's decision to create Brasilia as the country's new capital city in 1952. At that time the area around the chosen site was virtually uninhabited.
- the development of mineral resources and energy supplies at such places as Carajas, Trombetas and Tucurui (page 97), and the government's attempts to settle landless farmers in the Amazon basin (page 98).

São Paulo and Rio de Janeiro have big, modern buildings which include hospitals, shops, cinemas and universities

The North-east of Brazil has one of the highest birth rates in the world. The average family size is eight people. There are too many of us to find jobs on the farms

Drought and poor soils mean we cannot grow enough food to feed ourselves and so we have to move to the city

We are farmers but many of us do not own any land, and if we do the plots are very small

We have learned some skills at school but we cannot use them in our local village

It is not far to the city so we can get work there and still visit our village

C

Activities

1 a) Which groups of immigrants to Brazil came from
   i) eastern Asia before AD 1400, ii) Africa,
   iii) Europe, iv) Asia during this century?
   b) Into which parts of Brazil did each of these four immigrant groups settle?

2 Make a copy of diagram **D**. Complete it to show why places in the south-east of Brazil are more densely populated than places in the north and west of Brazil, by adding descriptions to the headings for **each** area.

3 a) i) Why have so many people moved from rural areas in Brazil into towns and cities?
   ii) What was Brazil's urban population in 1940, 1970 and 1990?
   b) How was the building of Brasilia meant to encourage people to move inland and away from the south-east coast?
   c) What two recent developments have encouraged people to move into the Amazon basin?

D

Decreases ← **Population density** → Increases

A — Amazon Basin and North-west Brazil

B — Central Brazil

C — South-east Brazil

- Climate and water supply
- Relief and drainage
- National resources
- Transport
- Services and amenities
- Government help

E

People living in urban areas (%)

Year	%
1940	32
1950	40
1960	42
1970	56
1980	68
1990	77
2000 (est)	82

Summary

The distribution of population in Brazil has mainly been influenced by physical factors and migration both into and within the country.

▶ Does Brazil have the characteristics of a developing country? ◀

We are all aware of different levels in development between places. We can see differences within a British city, between regions in the United Kingdom and in the European Union, and between countries across the world. Perhaps the sharpest contrast in development made by people is when they place the countries of the world into one of two groups so that each country is said to be either 'economically more developed' or 'economically less developed'. The placing of a country in either of these two groups depends upon certain characteristics. These characteristics include

- economic factors which explain the wealth of a country e.g. Gross National Product (GNP) (page 108), the development of industry and the level and type of trade.
- social factors which describe the standard of living and quality of life in a country, e.g. population growth, health care and education.

Unfortunately, when considering these characteristics it is all too easy to generalise and to build up a **negative**, and often incorrect, **perception** of an economically developing country (diagram **A**). We often only hear about these countries through the media during times of a major disaster such as drought or civil war. When the disaster passes and conditions in the country improve, it is 'forgotten' as it is no longer considered to be 'news-worthy'. Perception is often very different to reality.

Brazil is grouped with the economically less developed countries, but is it one of them? How does it measure up to the characteristics of an economically developing country as listed in diagram **A**? How does it compare with other countries in the world (table **B**)?

A

B

1990	GNP (US$)	Birth rate	Death rate	Infant mortality rate	Population under the age of 15 (%)	Life expectancy	People in primary jobs (%)	Energy consumption per person	Urban dwellers (%)	People per doctor	Adult literacy	Trade balance
Japan	23 730	12	8	5	35	79	7	403	78	780	99	Surplus
USA	21 000	14	9	8	27	76	2	1013	75	520	99	Deficit
UK	14 570	14	12	8	23	76	2	503	94	650	99	Deficit
France	17 830	13	10	7	23	76	6	395	74	540	99	Deficit
Brazil	2550	26	8	57	42	66	25	80	83	1660	78	Surplus
Mexico	1990	27	5	36	44	70	31	169	77	2010	90	Deficit
Egypt	630	31	11	57	40	61	41	75	55	970	45	Deficit
Kenya	380	47	10	64	39	61	77	11	32	7870	60	Deficit
India	350	31	12	88	39	60	72	31	34	3690	57	Deficit
Bangladesh	180	41	14	108	38	53	69	7	18	7810	33	Deficit

Twelve characteristics of development are listed in table **B**. Of these twelve, Brazil appears to fall into the category of 'economically less developed' on four occasions, into 'economically more developed' on three and is borderline between them on the remaining five (diagram **C**). Indeed when it comes to trade, Brazil has had a surplus since 1982 This means that it has earned more money from exporting its raw materials and manufactured goods to other countries than it has spent on imports. In 1990, the date of the figures in table **B**, Brazil and Japan were the only countries to show a trade surplus. In contrast, the USA, UK and France all had, like the economically less developed countries, a trade deficit. It is often difficult, and misleading, therefore to label a country as being either economically 'more developed' or 'less developed'.

Brazil experienced a so-called 'economic miracle' in the 1960s and 1970s. During this time it developed large scale industries, began to utilise its energy resources and increased its GNP. However, just as economic development is not even across the world, neither is it even within a country. Although Brazil's 'economic miracle' created many new industrial jobs in the country, its benefits were mainly confined to the government, large businesses and overseas multinational companies. The improvement in economic wealth was not shared equally between all the regions and people within the country (pages 102 and 103), while the money borrowed to pay for new developments has left Brazil deep in debt (pages 104 and 105).

Level of development	Where does Brazil fit?
Least economically developed countries	No similarities
Below average economically	Population aged under 15 years. Energy consumption. Birth rate. Infant mortality
Average economic development	GNP. People per doctor. Adult literacy
Above average economically developed countries	Life expectancy. People with primary jobs (%)
Most economically developed countries	Death rate. Urban dwellers (%). Trade balance

C

D

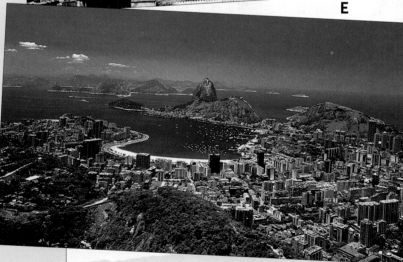

E

Activities

1 Diagram **A** makes fifteen points. Explain why each point is characteristic of an economically less developed country.

2 Table **B** gives twelve differences in the level of development between ten selected countries. Using this, and table **C**,
   a) list the characteristics which Brazil shares with countries which are said to be
      i) economically less developed
      ii) economically more developed.
   b) Why is it often difficult to label a country as being either 'economically more developed' or 'economically less developed'?

3 a) Write down the first ten things you think of about Brazil. These are likely to be your perceptions of the country.
   b) Which of these perceptions are negative (bad) points and which are positive (good) points?
   c) Photos **D** and **E** were both taken in Rio de Janeiro.
      i) How does photo **D** confirm the often negative perceptions of an economically less developed country?
      ii) How does photo **E** show that there are also many positive characteristics about economically less developed countries?

Summary Individual countries have different levels of economic development and so are referred to as being either economically 'more' or 'less' developed. While Brazil is commonly regarded to be part of the 'less developed' world, it shows several characteristics usually associated with 'more developed' countries.

Why has economic development in Brazil been uneven?

Economic development is rarely evenly distributed whether it be in a city or at a regional, national or international level. Growth and wealth become concentrated in a few favoured locations (the **core**) leaving other places relatively poor and underdeveloped in comparison (the **periphery**) (page 90). In the case of a country, the core is likely to contain the most jobs (usually in the secondary and tertiary sectors), the most developed transport system, and the best housing and services. It is also likely to have the highest standard of living. In most countries the level of prosperity and economic development decreases rapidly with distance from the core (map **A**). The poorest regions are therefore usually found towards the periphery of the country. Mainly due to a lack of jobs (other than those in the primary sector), people will migrate from the more 'rural' periphery regions to the more urbanised, industrial core.

A

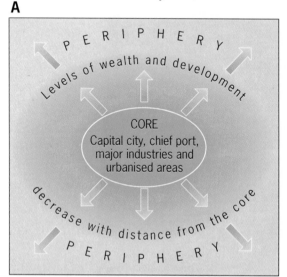

B

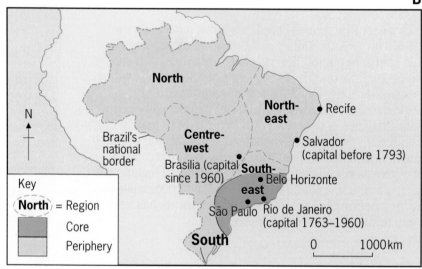

C São Paulo

D Favelas in Salvador

Regional imbalance in Brazil

During the early years of Portuguese colonial rule, the North-east became the wealthiest region of Brazil (map **B**). Its wealth was based on plantation crops, especially sugar cane. Salvador (Brazil's first capital) and Recife grew as ports, exporting sugar and receiving large numbers of European immigrants together with slaves brought from Africa. However, it has been the South-east region where, and especially since 1950, industrialisation, urbanisation and the creation of jobs and wealth has been the most rapid. Today the North-east has 30 per cent of Brazil's population but only 14 per cent of the country's wealth compared with the South-east where 42 per cent of the population now live and which has 64 per cent of the nation's wealth. The South-east is therefore the core region in Brazil (photo **C** and Fact file **E**) with the North-east, together with the North, forming the periphery (photo **D** and Fact file **F**).

Fact file E
South-east Brazil – the core

The initial development of the South-east was centred on coffee growing (São Paulo), gold and diamond prospecting (Minas Gerais) and their export through the natural port of Rio de Janeiro. Real growth followed with the mining of iron ore, the production of steel, and the manufacture of ships and cars. Hydro-electricity, produced locally, and oil, imported and refined at Rio, provided the necessary supply of energy. The region has become Brazil's centre of commerce, education, administration, transport and culture. The prospect of more and better paid jobs, a more reliable food supply, improved services (schools and hospitals) and the perception of the 'bright city lights' have all acted like a magnet to attract many people who previously lived in the surrounding rural areas. The region has received most government and foreign investment and has, despite the large number of people living in favelas and on the streets, the highest standard of living in the country.

Fact file F
North-east Brazil – the periphery

Most people are subsistence farmers or are landless sharecroppers who farm the land for someone else and in return receive a share of the produce. The soils, once used to produce plantation crops, are now mainly exhausted and eroded. The poor soils and frequent drought mean that crop yields are often insufficient to feed the local population. Where soils are better, the crops grown are usually for export (sugar cane and cocoa) rather than for home consumption. The high birth rate and lack of natural resources means that the region is overpopulated. Although there is one large hydro-electric power station in the region (Paulo Afonso), energy supplies are insufficient for domestic use or the development of industry. The lack of government and foreign investment has meant that transport systems and industry has not developed and services have not been provided. The lack of jobs, services and a guaranteed food supply has meant the migration of thousands of people from the region. Many have moved to the South-east and a few have been resettled in the North.

E

F

Activities

1 a) The core region has the greatest level of urbanisation in a country together with the most industries and services. With reference to table **G** give
   i) one piece of evidence that more people live in urban areas;
   ii) two pieces of evidence that there is more industry;
   iii) three pieces of evidence that health care (services) is better;
   iv) one piece of evidence that education is better;
   v) two pieces of evidence that there are better household amenities;
   vi) two pieces of evidence that the standard of living is higher in South-east Brazil (the core) than in North-east Brazil (the periphery).
   b) i) Why is the South-east of Brazil more economically developed than the North-east of Brazil?
   ii) Is it true that all of South-east Brazil has a high standard of living?

Brazil	South-east	North-east
Population density	63 per km²	25 per km²
Birth rate	22	48
Infant mortality rate	49	109
Life expectancy	63	48
People per doctor	875	2150
Adult literacy (%)	72	39
Brazil's industrial production (%)	56	16
People employed in industry (%)	70	10
Brazil's energy consumption (%)	71	13
Urban dwellers (%)	84	47
With electricity (%)	82	15
Clean water (%)	64	23
Car ownership (%)	66	10

G

Summary

Wealth and economic development are rarely spread out evenly. Parts of South-east Brazil are as well-off as many economically more developed countries. Other parts of South-east Brazil have, like the North-east, a very low standard of living.

How has internal investment affected Brazil's economic development?

Economic development and growth needs capital and technology, two commodities which are not readily available to economically less developed countries. Development, therefore, has to rely upon assistance either in limited amounts from their own government or, as is more usual, from overseas. Brazil's government, together with the Bank of Brasil, helped to build the state-owned steelworks at Volta Redonda and to form the state-controlled Petrobras petroleum company. These early schemes were expensive and tended to concentrate industrial expansion in the South-east at the expense of other parts of the country.

Brasilia

Many Brazilians expressed concern over the speed of economic development and population and urban growth in a triangular area which was bounded by São Paulo, Rio de Janeiro and Belo Horizonte. This growth led to an increasing gap in wealth between the South-east and other Brazilian regions. In 1952 the Brazilian Congress agreed to create a new capital city. The site chosen was uninhabited, was almost equidistant from all the regional capitals and was 1200 kilometres inland from the existing capital of Rio de Janeiro. Building work began in 1957 and Brasilia was inaugurated as capital in 1960. The main hope was that Brasilia would lead to the opening up of the more central parts of the country and so spread out Brazil's economic growth more evenly. Although Brasilia's population had reached 1.9 million by 1990, its economy was based on commerce and administration rather than industry (photo **A**). Many top business people and politicians still prefer to live in Rio de Janeiro or São Paulo and to commute to work during the week. Brasilia, a city built for the motorist, has become the focus for new roads which lead away in all directions.

Regional development

During the mid-1960s the Brazilian government set up five regional development agencies. One of these, SUDAM, became responsible for developing Amazonia and improving its social and economic conditions. The agency realised that the region could not be developed without improved accessibility and so, in 1968, it financed a route through the rainforest for the Trans Amazonian Highway (photo **B**). This, and later highways, became a 'growth corridor' along which landless farmers from the North-east region (page 103) were re-settled as 'colonists' (photo **C**). Although the colonists were given land to farm, the settlement programme has not been a success. The traditional method of farming in the rainforest had been shifting cultivation (page 95). This was because, once the forest had been cleared, the heavy rain soon leached and eroded the soil (page 40). While the Amerindian shifting cultivators could then move to a new site in the forest, the 'colonists' could not. Consequently as crop yields fell and feelings of isolation grew, many colonists have abandoned their new farms and moved to the large urban centres on the coast and in the South-east.

A Brasilia

B The Trans Amazonian Highway

In 1975 the Brazilian government introduced a Second National Development Plan called, in this region, **Polamazonia**. Fifteen 'growth poles' were created in the region (map **E**). At each growth pole the government, often with help from multinational companies, invested large sums of money to try to generate economic activity. The hope was that as each centre developed, growth would extend outwards into the surrounding areas. Developments have included highways, a free port, mining (iron ore and bauxite – photo **D**), agriculture (cattle ranching), industry (timber and steel) and the production of hydro-electricity (map **E**). As always with development schemes, there are advantages and disadvantages. Polamazonia is credited with creating many new jobs, generating wealth for many Brazilian-owned companies and helping the country to achieve a trade surplus (page 107). It has also been blamed for destroying large areas of rainforest and the traditional Amerindian way of life.

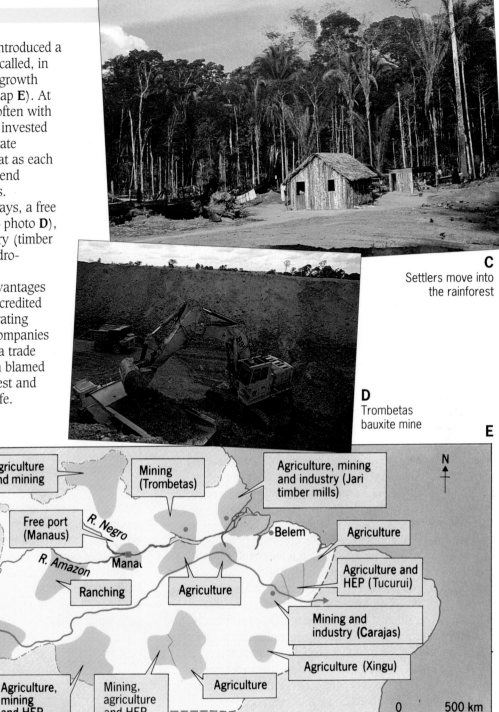

C
Settlers move into the rainforest

D
Trombetas bauxite mine

E

Key
---.--- Brazilian border
- - - - SUDAM's border
Polamazonia projects

Free port – an area where goods can be made or assembled without payment of import or export duties

Trans Amazonia Highway

HEP – Hydro-electric power

Agriculture and mining

Mining (Trombetas)

Agriculture, mining and industry (Jari timber mills)

Free port (Manaus)

R. Negro

Belem

Agriculture

R. Amazon   Manaus

Agriculture and HEP (Tucurui)

Ranching

Agriculture

Mining and industry (Carajas)

Agriculture (Xingu)

Ranching

Agriculture, mining and HEP

Mining, agriculture and HEP

Agriculture

N

0   500 km

Activities

1 a) Why was there a need for development in other regions in Brazil, apart from the South-east?
   b) Give three reasons why the Brazilian government created the new capital of Brasilia.

2 a) What was SUDAM?
   b) Why were growth corridors created? How successful have they been?

   c) What were the main aims of Polamazonia?
   d) Describe five different types of economic development which have taken place under Polamazonia. In what ways have these developments been successful and what problems have they created?

Summary

The amount of government (inward) investment can greatly influence the speed and type of economic development of an economically developing country.

How has foreign investment affected Brazil's economic development?

Many economically developing countries have come to rely upon aid. Aid is the giving of resources by one country, or an organisation, to another country. Aid can include money, goods, food, technology and people. Developing countries may seek aid for these reasons.

- To try to improve their standard of living - although this type of aid is often spent on prestigious schemes (e.g. hydro-electricity schemes) which benefit relatively few people within the country.
- To pay off trade debts - most developing countries do not make enough money from their exports (usually primary products) to pay for their imports (usually manufactured goods).
- Following disasters - many developing countries are prone either to natural disasters (e.g. drought and earthquakes) or human-induced disasters (e.g desertification and civil war).

The three main types of aid are described in diagram **A**. Unfortunately the giving of aid is complicated and controversial, because it often does not benefit the country or the people to whom it is given.

After 1964, foreign banks and multinational companies perceived that Brazil had a huge potential for industrial growth. Foreign banks became increasingly prepared to loan money to the Brazilian government while multinational companies invested money in developing the country's mineral reserves, energy resources and industry (photo **B**). Both the banks and the multinational companies assumed that, as Brazil developed economically, they would get their money back and make a handsome profit. These loans and investments have had mixed effects upon the Brazilian economy. The Brazilian government, using bank loans, has financed several successful state companies, including Petrobras and Telebras, while multinationals, especially those connected with oil and cars, have created jobs and wealth (table **C**). However, although Brazil has become the most industrialised and one of the better off economically less developed countries, it has done so at the expense of creating a huge national debt (graph **D** and extract **E**).

A

Bilateral aid is when one country gives resources directly to another country. It is usually given 'with strings attached' which gives the donor some control over the recipient. E.g. the recipient **must** buy manufactured goods from the donor. Recipient countries usually fall deeply into debt.

Multilateral aid is given by international organisations such as the World Bank or EU Development Fund. Often these organisations, based in 'rich' countries, hold back if they disagree with the economic or political system of the recipient country.

Voluntary aid is given by organisations such as Oxfam, Action Aid and Intermediate Technology. There are no political ties. Money is spent on sustainable, small-scale projects more appropriate to the needs and technology of recipient countries.

During the 1980s Brazil had to borrow more money just to repay interest rates on earlier loans. At the same time economic growth and the creation of wealth was not evenly distributed between regions and people (pages 102-103). As in many economically developing countries the gaps between the rich and the poor and between the core and the periphery have grown more rapidly than in the economically developed world.

C

Rank	Company	Field of business	Ownership
1	Petrobras	Petroleum	Brazil
2	Pao de Açucar	Supermarkets	Brazil
3	Shell	Petroleum	UK/Netherlands
4	Telebras	Telecommunications	Brazil
5	Texaco Brazil	Petroleum	USA
6	Volkswagen do Brasil	Cars	Germany
7	Esso Brasileira	Petroleum	USA
8	Sousa Cruz	Beverages, tobacco	UK
9	Vale do Rio Dole	Mining (Carajas)	Brazil
10	Mendes Junior	Machinery	Brazil
11	General Motors	Cars	USA
12	Copersucar (fuel for cars)	Sugar, alcohol	Brazil

B

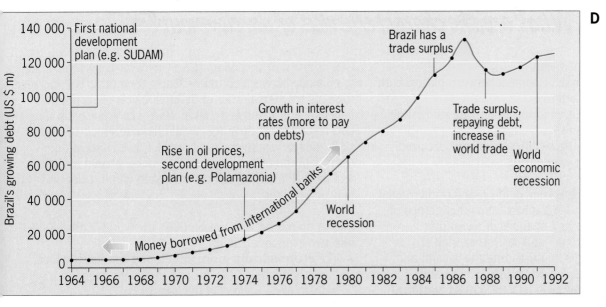

D

Brazil's growing debt (US $ m)

- First national development plan (e.g. SUDAM)
- Rise in oil prices, second development plan (e.g. Polamazonia)
- Money borrowed from international banks
- Growth in interest rates (more to pay on debts)
- World recession
- Brazil has a trade surplus
- Trade surplus, repaying debt, increase in world trade
- World economic recession

(Years: 1964–1992)

E

Economic miracle and international debt

Between 1964 and 1974 the military government, supported by the USA, developed policies to make Brazil prosperous and powerful. During this period, known as the 'economic miracle', landless peasants, used as cheap labour, made this aim seem as possibility. European and American banks encouraged this economic growth by offering large loans with low interest rates. These were used to finance ambitious, often ill-founded industrial and agricultural projects. Multinational companies set up industries but most of their profits were taken out of the country.

Imports of cheap oil helped this process of economic expansion, but, in the mid-70s oil prices rose steeply, so increasing import bills. As a result of Western government policies, interest rates on the loans increased and the prices for Brazil's exports on the world market fell. Rich countries limited the amount of Brazilian manufactured goods that they imported. All these pressures were outside the control of the Brazilian government. Brazil tried to bridge the gap between earnings and debt payments by borrowing more money over short periods, but this increased the government's debts even further. Today, Brazil's external debt has now reached $US119 billion, with little possibility of full payment.

Source:Brazil Country Profile, ActionAid

AID · DEBT REPAYMENTS LOW COMMODITY PRICES

Activities

1 a) Why do many economically developing countries seek aid?
   b) What are the differences between bilateral, multilateral and voluntary aid?
   c) Which of the three types of aid do you consider to be the best for the receiving country? Give reasons for your answer.

2 a) Why were foreign banks prepared to make loans, and multinational companies to invest in Brazil after 1964?
   b) How has Brazil benefitted from these loans and investments?
   c) What problems have resulted from these loans and investments?
   d) Why did Brazil's debt increase rapidly between 1974 and 1986?
   e) Although Brazil has had a trade surplus since 1986 (graph **F**), why has it been unable to reduce its debt?

F

Brazil's balance of trade (US $ m). +8.3 = trade balance surplus (%). Exports / Imports.

Year	Surplus
1986	+8.3
1987	+11.2
1988	+19.2
1989	+16.1
1990	+10.7
1991	+10.6

Summary

Brazil needed foreign loans and investment to stimulate economic development. Economic growth has, however, led to a large national debt and an increasing gap between Brazil's rich and poor.

▶ What are the characteristics of development? ◀

Geographers are concerned with
- differences in levels in development between places, both within and between countries.
- mapping these differences to see if there are recognisable patterns in development.
- trying to explain why these differences have occurred, and how they may be evened out.

The term 'development' has been defined, and is interpreted, in many different ways. Geographers, and other groups of people, find it difficult to find methods of measuring development. The traditional, and easiest, method of comparing development is by measuring the 'wealth and economic growth' of a region or country. The wealth of a country is measured in terms of its GNP (**Gross National Product**). The GNP per capita is the total value of goods produced and services provided by a country in a given year, divided by the number of people living in that country.

GNP is given in US dollars (US $) to allow easy comparisons to be made between countries. Table **B** on page 100 included the GNP for 10 countries at different levels of economic development. It showed that in 1990 every person in the UK, regardless of their age, would have received 14 570 US$ had the wealth created in the UK been shared out evenly. In the real world, wealth is never shared out evenly and so GNP hides differences in wealth within cities and between regions.

Map **A** shows how, based on GNP, the world can be divided into two economic groups.
- The **economically more developed** countries, which have the highest GNP, include the richer, more industrialised nations of the 'North'.
- The **economically less developed** countries, with the lowest GNP, include the poorer, less industrialised nations of the 'South'.

A

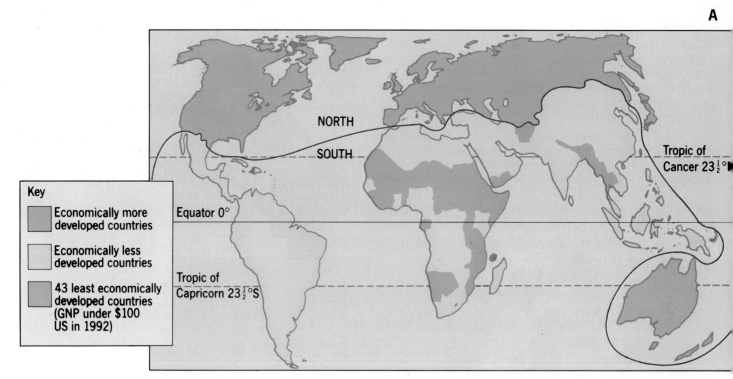

Key
- Economically more developed countries
- Economically less developed countries
- 43 least economically developed countries (GNP under $100 US in 1992)

NORTH
SOUTH
Tropic of Cancer 23½°
Equator 0°
Tropic of Capricorn 23½°S

To many people living in a western, industrialised country such as the UK, economic development has been associated with a growth in wealth. This suggested that the GNP of a country had to increase if the standard of living and quality of life of its inhabitants was to improve. More recently the meaning of the term 'development' has been widened to include various social, health and educational indicators. However, as shown in diagram **B** opposite, and in table **B** on page 100, these indicators are themselves usually dependent upon the wealth of a country. Economically less developed countries are perceived, in comparison to economically more developed countries, as having smaller volumes of trade and a trade deficit; more jobs in the primary sector and fewer in the secondary and tertiary sectors; higher birth, death and infant mortality rates; shorter life expectancy; a lower level of literacy and relatively few doctors per size of population.

B

		Developing countries	Developed countries
Jobs	 Number of jobs in the primary, secondary and tertiary sectors, expressed as a percentage	Most jobs in primary sector (highest percentage in farming). Relatively few in secondary and tertiary sectors.	Few jobs in the primary sector. Larger number in the secondary sector. Highest percentage in the tertiary sector.
Trade	 Volume (amount), value and type of trade	Small in volume and value. Mainly raw materials (minerals and foodstuffs which are cheap to buy).	Large volume and value. Mainly manufactured goods (expensive to buy).
Population	 Birth rate – number of births per 1000 people Death rate – number of deaths per 1000 people Infant mortality rate – number of babies out of every 1000 born alive who die before the age of one Life expectancy – age a person born in a country can expect to live	High birth rate (falling). Relatively high death rate (falling). High infant mortality rate (falling slightly). Short life expectancy (increasing).	Low birth rate (steady). Low death rate (steady). Low infant mortality rate (steady). Long life expectancy (increasing).
Health	 Number of people to every doctor	Few doctors, nurses and hospitals. Each doctor may have several thousand patients.	More doctors, nurses and hospitals. Each doctor may only have several hundred patients.
Education	 Level of literacy – the percentage of adults able to read and write	Insufficient money for full time education. Low percentage of literate adults, especially among women.	Full time education. High percentage of literate adults including women.

Activities

1 a) What do you understand by the term 'development'?
   b) Why is development hard to define?
   c) What is gross national product (GNP)?
   d) What is the GNP for each of the USA, the UK, Brazil, Kenya and India?
   e) Why do the USA and the UK have a higher GNP than Kenya and India?

   f) Describe the location and distribution of the economically less developed countries.

2 Name six indicators, other than GNP, which can be used to show differences in levels of development between regions and countries.

Summary

GNP is the most frequent method used to show differences in development between places. Development can also be measured using social, health and educational indicators.

▶ *Is there a link between GNP and development?* ◀

Many of the characteristics (page 108) applied to economically less developed countries are often linked to their GNP. How justifiable and accurate are these statements? For example do birth and infant mortality rates decrease and does life expectancy increase as the GNP (wealth) of a country increases? It is possible, by using a **scattergraph**, to see whether there is a close link, or relationship, between GNP and the various characteristics of development.

Table **A** gives three variables. These variables are the GNP, life expectancy and the birth rate for ten selected countries which are at different stages of economic development. The resultant graphs shows a scatter of ten crosses to which a 'best fit line' has been added. The resultant best fit line does not pass through all of the points on the graph, but it has been drawn as close as possible to all of them. The closer the scatter of crosses is to a straight line, the closer is the relationship between the two variables.

If, as in the first graph, the best fit line goes from the bottom left to the top right then the relationship, or correlation, between the two variables is said to be **positive** (diagram **B(a)**). This means that 'as the GNP (one variable) of a country increases then so too does the life expectancy (the second variable)'.

If, as on the second graph, the best fit line goes from top left to bottom right then, while there is still a close relationship between the two variables, this time the correlation is said to be **negative** (diagram **B(c)**). This is because 'as the GNP (one variable) increases then the birth rate (the second variable) decreases'.

Occasionally a scattergraph may show one or more points to lie a long way from the best fit line (diagram **B(d)**). These points are called anomalies because they do not fit with the usual trend or pattern. Usually there is a specific reason for an anomaly. For example, a country may have a higher than expected birth rate as religious beliefs may be contrary to birth control.

A

Country	Variables		
	GNP (US$)	Life expectancy	Birth rate
Japan	23 730	79	12
USA	21 000	76	14
UK	14 570	76	14
France	17 830	76	13
Brazil	2550	66	26
Mexico	1990	70	27
Egypt	630	61	31
Kenya	380	61	47
India	350	60	31
Bangladesh	180	53	41

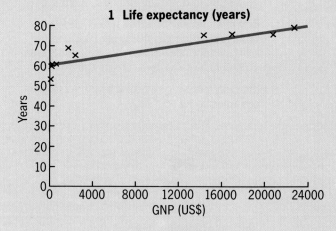

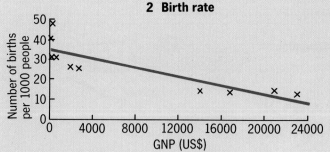

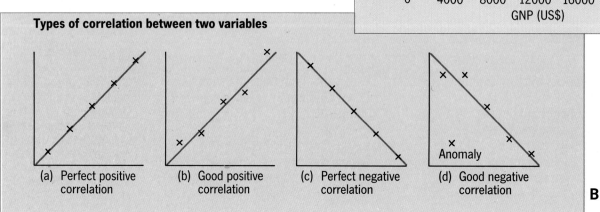

Types of correlation between two variables

(a) Perfect positive correlation

(b) Good positive correlation

(c) Perfect negative correlation

(d) Good negative correlation

Anomaly

B

Development and literacy

Table **B** on page 100 gave the adult literacy rates for ten countries at different stages of economic development. It does not need a scattergraph to see the close positive relationship between the two variables of adult literacy and GNP. The higher the GNP the greater the number of adults who can read and write, since high levels of illiteracy are both a cause and a result of poverty. However, adult literacy figures, especially those for the less economically developed countries, hide the fact that illiteracy rates for women are usually much higher than those for men. Map **C** shows that female illiteracy rates are highest in Africa, where women have spent on average only one year at school, and in southern Asia. Some of the explanations for Africa's high illiteracy rates are given in diagram **D**. How the education of women helps a country to develop is described on page 115.

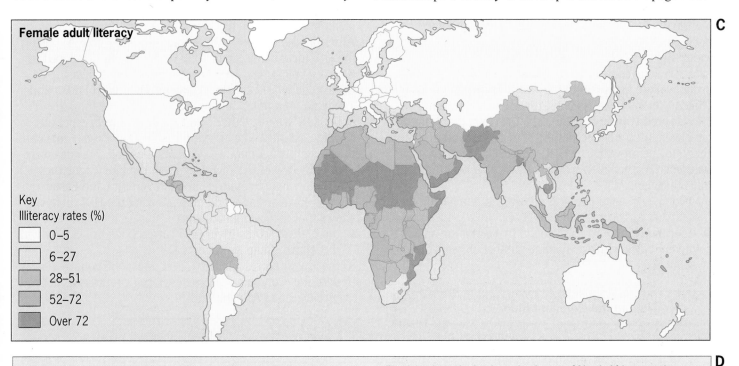

C

Female adult literacy

Key
Illiteracy rates (%)

- 0–5
- 6–27
- 28–51
- 52–72
- Over 72

D

Women are responsible for family care. The majority are also unpaid farmers who have to collect water and fuelwood, and do the cooking. This leaves little time for education. In countries like Ghana and Kenya many sustainable appropriate technology schemes are run by women.

The Islamic male-dominated cultures of North Africa see the role of women as limited to work in the home. Consequently education is thought to be unnecessary. South of the Equator, women are so occupied in farming and trading that they are prevented from gaining an education. This is due to the constraints of poverty, time and tradition.

Activities

1. a) Draw a scattergraph to show any possible relationship between GNP and the percentage of people employed in agriculture. The figures are in table **B** on page 100.
   b) Is the relationship (correlation) positive or negative? Explain what this means.

2. a) What is the relationship between GNP and illiteracy?
   b) Why are female illiteracy rates so high in Africa?

Summary

Scattergraphs show relationships between variables e.g. GNP and life expectancy, birth rates and the numbers employed in agriculture.

▶ How can development be measured other than by GNP? ◀

It has already been pointed out that GNP provides the easiest method of measuring, and the simplest way of comparing, different levels of development (page 108). However, it is increasingly argued that the term 'development' has a wider meaning that just 'wealth'.

During the 1980s the Overseas Development Council (ODC) suggested the physical quality of life index (PQLI). This index replaced GNP (an economic measure) with literacy rates, life expectancy and infant mortality (three social/welfare measures). This was followed, in 1990, by the United Nations Development Programme's **'Human Development Index'** (**HDI**). The UN claim that human development is a better method of measuring development than income growth. The HDI gives each country a score based on its population's combined income, length of life and education.

- Income per capita (GNP) is adjusted to purchasing power, i.e. what an income will actually buy in a country.
- Educational attainment is found by combining adult literacy rates with the average number of years of schooling.

- Life expectancy is regarded as the best measure of a country's health and safety.

Each variable is given a score ranging from 1 (the best) to 0 (the poorest). The HDI is the average score, also ranging from 1 to 0, of the three variables. The latest UN figures put Japan at the top with a score of 0.993 and Guinea (West Africa) at the bottom with a score of 0.045 (table **A**). Using the HDI means that Japan (0.993) is twice as developed as Kenya (0.081). The HDI suggests how poor a measure of development GNP can be. Countries such as Sri Lanka and Tanzania rank much higher in the HDI league than they do in the GNP league. Other countries do less well, especially Middle East oil producing countries such as Saudi Arabia and the United Arab Emirates. Whereas these oil countries were near to the top of the GNP league, in the HDI league they rank below many countries in Latin America and Eastern Europe. Even so the world map showing the HDI (map **C**) shows that those countries with

- the highest scores (over 0.9) correspond very closely with the 'North' (map **A**, page 108).
- the lowest scores (under 0.25) correspond equally closely with the economically less developed countries as defined by GNP (map **A**, page 108).

A

Human Development Index

Rank order	Country	Life expectancy at birth (years)	Adult literacy rate (%)	Years of schooling (average)	Real GNP per capita (PPP$*)
1	Japan	78.6	99.0	10.7	17 616
2	Canada	77.0	99.0	12.1	19 232
3	Norway	77.1	99.0	11.6	16 028
4	Switzerland	77.4	99.0	11.1	20 874
5	Sweden	77.4	99.0	11.1	17 014
6	USA	75.9	99.0	12.3	21 449
7	Australia	76.5	99.0	11.5	16 051
8	France	76.4	99.0	11.6	17 405
9	Netherlands	77.2	99.0	10.6	15 695
10	United Kingdom	75.7	99.0	11.5	15 804
12	Germany	75.2	99.0	11.1	18 213
22	Italy	76.0	97.1	7.3	15 890
23	Spain	77.0	97.5	6.8	11 723
37	Russian Federation	69.3	94.0	9.0	7 968
48	Poland	71.8	96.0	8.0	4 237
53	Mexico	69.7	87.6	4.7	5 918
70	Brazil	65.6	81.1	3.9	4 718
84	Saudi Arabia	64.5	62.4	3.7	10 989
101	China	70.1	73.3	4.8	1 990
124	Egypt	60.3	48.4	2.8	1 988
129	Kenya	59.2	49.1	2.7	1 921
132	Pakistan	57.7	34.8	1.9	1 862
134	India	59.1	48.2	2.4	1 072
142	Nigeria	51.5	50.7	1.2	1 215
147	Bangladesh	57.8	35.3	2.0	872
170	Burkina Faso	48.2	18.2	0.1	618
171	Afghanistan	42.5	29.4	0.8	714
172	Sierra Leone	42.0	20.7	0.9	1 086
173	Guinea	43.5	24.0	0.8	501

*Purchasing power parity in US dollars
All figures are from 1990

B

Top developing nations (overall ranking)

1 Barbados (2)
2 Hong Kong (24)
3 Cyprus (27)
4 Uruguay (30)
5 Trinidad and Tobago (31)
6 Bahamas (32)
7 South Korea (33)
8 Chile (30)
9 Costa Rica (42)
10 Singapore (43)

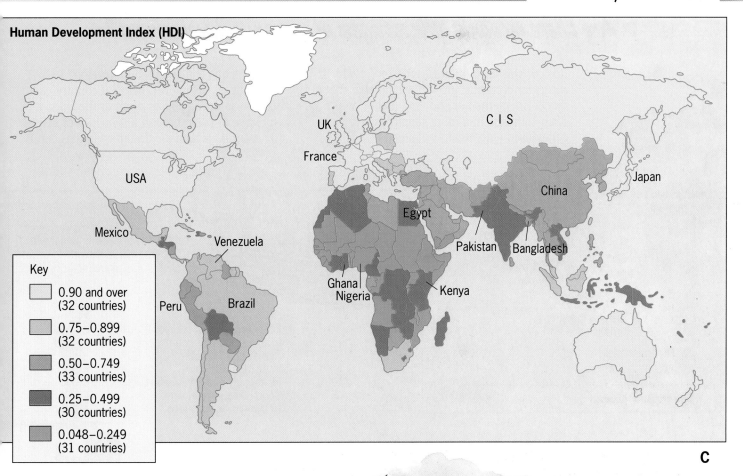

Human Development Index (HDI)

Key

☐	0.90 and over (32 countries)
☐	0.75–0.899 (32 countries)
☐	0.50–0.749 (33 countries)
☐	0.25–0.499 (30 countries)
☐	0.048–0.249 (31 countries)

C

D

The HDI can also be used to expose inequalities within a country as well as inequalities between countries. For example when the HDI is calculated for Black communities in the USA, it gives them a similar score to people living in Trinidad (table **B**).

The HDI is not without its critics who claim that the index should also include a measure of human rights and freedom. The UN has responded by arguing that human freedom is difficult and too volatile to measure. The HDI will serve its purpose if it shows where poverty is worst, and if it stimulates debate about where aid, trade and foreign debt reduction should best be focused.

Activities

1 a) Why did the United Nations suggest the Human Development Index (HDI)?
   b) Which three variables are used to determine the HDI?
   c) How is the HDI worked out?
   d) In what ways is the HDI a better guide to development than the more traditional use of GNP?

2 a) Describe carefully the location of those countries with an HDI of
   i)   over 0.9,
   ii) between 0.5 and 0.9,
   iii) under 0.5.
   b) How do these locations compare with a map showing GNP (page 108)?

Summary

The Human Development Index (HDI) has extended the meaning of development to include real income, education and life expectancy. Even so there are considerable similarities between the GNP and HDI maps.

► Are there recognisable stages in economic development? ◄

Rostow was an economist who proposed a model for economic growth. Remember that a model is a method of showing reality, which is often complex, in a more simplified and generalised way. Rostow claimed that all countries had the potential to develop economically. However, before a country can become as developed as Japan or the USA, it will have to pass through a sequence of stages (diagram **A**) which are described in diagram **B**.

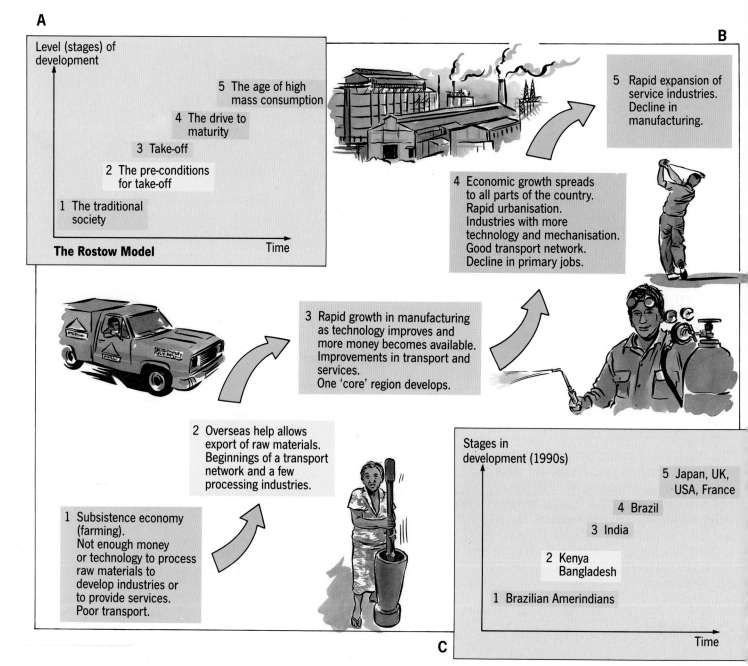

A

Level (stages) of development

5 The age of high mass consumption

4 The drive to maturity

3 Take-off

2 The pre-conditions for take-off

1 The traditional society

The Rostow Model

Time

B

5 Rapid expansion of service industries. Decline in manufacturing.

4 Economic growth spreads to all parts of the country. Rapid urbanisation. Industries with more technology and mechanisation. Good transport network. Decline in primary jobs.

3 Rapid growth in manufacturing as technology improves and more money becomes available. Improvements in transport and services. One 'core' region develops.

2 Overseas help allows export of raw materials. Beginnings of a transport network and a few processing industries.

1 Subsistence economy (farming). Not enough money or technology to process raw materials to develop industries or to provide services. Poor transport.

C

Stages in development (1990s)

5 Japan, UK, USA, France

4 Brazil

3 India

2 Kenya Bangladesh

1 Brazilian Amerindians

Time

Rostow's model, like other models, is open to criticism. He claimed that each country needed an injection of money before 'take off' could begin. However, it is now recognised that, despite financial aid, many countries are unlikely to become industrialised and economically developed. This may be due to a combination of a lack of raw materials, capital and technology as well as to a rapid growth in their population. Diagram **C** suggests, using Rostow's model, the stage of development reached by a selection of countries.

How can the quality of life in economically developing countries be improved?

Two methods by which economically developing countries may try to improve their quality of life is to raise their standards of education, especially for women, and to extend appropriate technology.

Education   Education can develop skills which can increase productivity in agriculture, industry and commerce. It can also raise self-confidence which allows people to try out new ideas. It is important that women are given the same educational opportunities as men (photo **D**). Agriculture is the back-bone of the economy in most of the economically less developed countries, and women are responsible for up to 70 per cent of the farm work. Education of women also leads to improvements in diet and hygiene, two factors which can reduce illness and improve health. It is an accepted fact that as female literacy increases, then birth rates and family size decrease.

Appropriate technology   Intermediate Technology is a British charitable organisation which works with people in economically less developed countries. It helps people, especially in rural areas, to acquire the tools and techniques needed if they are to work themselves out of poverty. Intermediate technology helps people to meet their basic needs in food, clothing, housing, farm equipment, energy and employment. Intermediate Technology uses local knowledge, and adds to it by providing technical advice, training, equipment, and financial support to help people to become more self-sufficient and

independent. The ideal is for local people to earn a surplus, however small, which can be invested in their subsistence farms and small scale businesses (photo **E**). Most of Intermediate Technology's projects are in response to local groups which are often, especially in Africa, run by women. Such projects should be sustainable and appropriate to the technology of the country involved.

D
Schoolgirls in Zimbabwe

E Women in Kenya unloading stoves from a kiln after firing

Activities

1   a) Draw a diagram to show the five stages of development in the Rostow model.
    b) Describe the level of development at each stage.
    c) At approximately which stage of development would you place the following countries: Italy, the CIS, Egypt, Mexico, Germany, Nigeria and Hong Kong?

2   a) Explain the importance of the following quotation: 'The need to educate women to the same level as men is seen by many as the greatest single way in which development can be encouraged'.
    b) What are the aims of Intermediate Technology?
    c) Why is their support often more valuable to an economically developing country than large loans given by the World Bank or a developed country?

Summary

Rostow's model suggests that a country has to pass through several stages before it becomes economically developed. The best opportunity for poorer countries to develop seems to lie with improved education and the use of appropriate technology.

▶ *How has trade affected development?* ◀

No country can provide everything that its inhabitants will want or need. To provide these needs a country has to **trade** with other countries. It has to buy (**import**) things which it is either short of, or which can be produced more cheaply elsewhere. These items may include foodstuffs, energy resources and manufactured goods. In order to buy these goods, a country has to sell (**export**) things of which it has a surplus, or which it can produce more cheaply than other countries. Ideally a country hopes to have a **trade surplus**.

This means that it earns more money from the goods which it exports than it has to spend on imports. A country with a trade surplus will become richer and can use the extra money to provide services and to widen its industries. Unfortunately it is impossible for every country to have a trade surplus. Those which have a **trade deficit** will remain poor, and will have insufficient money to develop new industries or to provide services. A country with a trade deficit spends more on imports than it earns from exports.

A

Trade and development

Colony 'developed' by colonial power

Exports 'cheap' raw materials to colonial power

e.g. foodstuffs and materials for industry – coffee, tea, tin, rubber, cotton

Colonial power imports cheap raw materials and processes them into manufactured goods

Exports 'expensive' manufactured goods

e.g. cars, machinery, clothes

A

B

To **other colonial powers** which today are the 'rich' economically more developed countries in the 'north'

To **former colonies** which today are the 'poor' economically less developed countries in the 'south'

World trade grew rapidly during colonial times. It was the richer countries in the 'North' which became the colonial powers. They 'developed' colonies in the 'South'.

B

Colonies provided raw materials (primary goods) for the colonial powers (diagram **A** and photo **B**). The colonial powers then either consumed these materials or processed them into manufactured goods. Many of the manufactured goods were then sold back to the colonies (photo **C**). The prices of primary goods are low in comparison to those of manufactured goods. The result has been a

- trade deficit for the former colonies leaving them as the economically less developed countries of the 'South'.
- trade surplus for the former colonial powers enabling them to become the economically more developed countries of the 'North'.

C

D

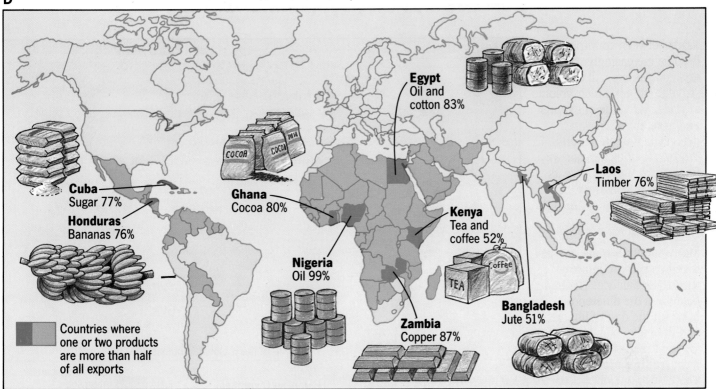

Egypt
Oil and cotton 83%

Laos
Timber 76%

Cuba
Sugar 77%

Honduras
Bananas 76%

Ghana
Cocoa 80%

Kenya
Tea and coffee 52%

Nigeria
Oil 99%

Bangladesh
Jute 51%

Zambia
Copper 87%

Countries where one or two products are more than half of all exports

Diagram **D** shows another problem faced by developing countries. Many of them, especially in Africa, rely heavily upon just one or two commodities to provide jobs at home and income from exports. When prices and demand for these products are high then the income earned by exporting them is also high. However, prices for primary goods are often fixed and kept low by the developed countries. Demand is more likely to fluctuate as it usually depends upon economic conditions in the developed countries. The economy of a developing country will therefore be seriously affected if

- a crop or mineral is over-produced,
- there is a decline in demand for a product, especially at times of world economic recession,
- a rival producer sells the item more cheaply,
- there is a crop failure or a mineral is used up.

Developing countries still have the largest percentage of their workforce in agriculture. However, farmers are often forced to grow crops for export, in order to earn money for the country, rather than to grow crops to feed themselves.

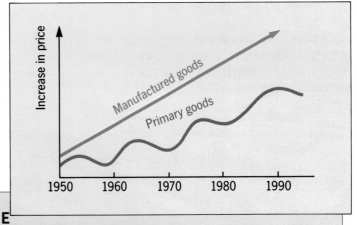

E

Activities

1 a) What is the difference between a trade surplus and a trade deficit?
   b) What type of goods are exported by countries in the
      i) South,
      ii) North?
   c) i) How does diagram **E** help to explain why the gap between rich and poor countries is getting wider?
      ii) Give four reasons for the price drop in primary products since 1990.

2 a) Name six countries that rely heavily upon the export of one or two commodities.
   b) Why do countries that depend mainly on one or two exports
      i) usually have a trade deficit,
      ii) find it difficult to improve their standard of living and quality of life?

Summary Countries trade to try to share out resources and to earn money. Countries which only export raw materials do not develop as quickly economically as countries which export manufactured goods.

▶ *How do government policies affect international trade?* ◀

A

Trade between countries has become increasingly complex and competitive. All countries strive to improve their volume of trade and value of exports and to reduce their dependency upon imports. Trade is seen as a major way for a country to improve its standard of living and, as a result, the quality of life of its inhabitants.

Many countries have grouped together to try to improve their trade balance. The trade balance is the difference between the cost of imports and the value of exports. By joining together countries form **trading blocs** (map **A**). The UK is a member of one of these blocs, the European Union (EU). One of the first aims of the EU was to try to improve trading links between member countries. This was achieved by eliminating customs duties previously paid on goods moved between member countries. This lowered the price of those goods making them cheaper and more competitive against goods from non-EU countries. Also, as the number of EU member countries has grown, so too has its internal market. The larger the internal market the greater the number of potential customers.

Map **B** shows that trade is not shared out equally between countries. Whereas the EU, the USA and Japan together are responsible for 62 per cent of the world trade total, the developing countries together only account for 20 per cent. Differences in trade are another reason why the gap in development between the rich countries and the poor countries continues to widen.

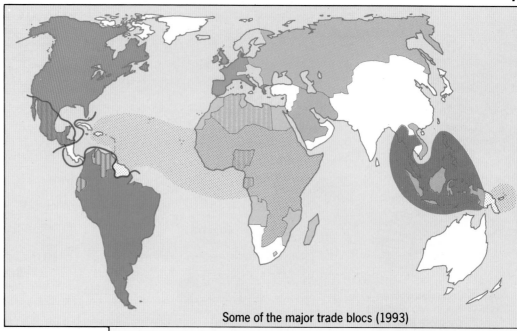

Some of the major trade blocs (1993)

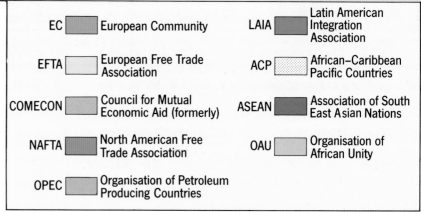

EC	European Community	LAIA	Latin American Integration Association	
EFTA	European Free Trade Association	ACP	African–Caribbean Pacific Countries	
COMECON	Council for Mutual Economic Aid (formerly)	ASEAN	Association of South East Asian Nations	
NAFTA	North American Free Trade Association	OAU	Organisation of African Unity	
OPEC	Organisation of Petroleum Producing Countries			

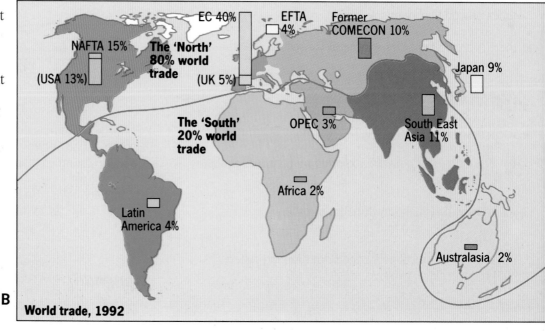

B **World trade, 1992**

NAFTA 15%
(USA 13%)
EC 40%
(UK 5%)
The 'North' 80% world trade
EFTA 4%
Former COMECON 10%
Japan 9%
The 'South' 20% world trade
OPEC 3%
South East Asia 11%
Africa 2%
Latin America 4%
Australasia 2%

In an ideal world there should be free trade between all countries. Free trade is when governments neither restrict nor encourage the movement of goods. In the real world of today, this rarely happens. Virtually all governments, and especially those of economically more developed countries, are involved in regulating overseas trade. This is done by creating trade barriers which, governments hope, will protect jobs and industries within their own country. The most common methods of affecting the levels and patterns of international trade are through **tariffs** and import **quotas**. The years of negotiations leading up to the GATT trade agreement of December 1993 (page 120) were centred on trying to remove trade restrictions. Economists claimed such an agreement would increase world trade, create more jobs and, even more important in the poorer countries, raise standards of living.

Tariffs, quotas, cartels and international commodity agreements

Tariffs are taxes or customs duties paid on imports. The exporter has to pay a percentage of the value of the goods to the importer. Importers sometimes add tariffs just to raise money, but usually it is to put up the price of imported goods so that they become more expensive and therefore harder to sell. Tariffs can therefore either reduce the cost of imports (helping the trade balance) or protect similar home-made goods.

Quotas limit the amount of goods which can be imported. At present, quotas tend to be restricted to primary goods and so work against the economically less developed countries.

Cartels occur when countries group together to set fixed prices for their product. Tariffs, quotas and cartels all work in favour of the 'rich' countries.

International commodity agreements, in contrast, are made by developing countries. They are made in an effort to stabilise prices and demand for individual primary commodities. The best known of these agreements was that made in 1960 by a group of oil producing countries which called themselves OPEC (map **A**). Other agreements have been made on commodities such as coffee, tin, cocoa and rubber.

Activities

1 a) Map **C** shows four trading blocks. For each trading bloc give
   i) its initials,   ii) its name in full,
   iii) the names of three member countries.
 b) Give two reasons why countries group together to form trading blocs.

2 Diagram **D** shows the volume of trade between the EU, the USA and Japan.
 a) What percentage of world trade is shared by the EU, USA and Japan?
 b) Of the three which has a
   i) trade surplus with the other two,
   ii) trade surplus with one and a trade deficit with the other,
   iii) trade deficit with the other two?

C

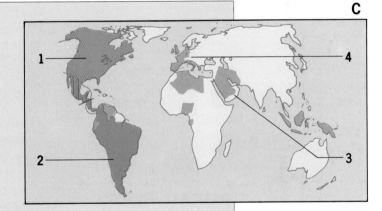

D

| US to Japan 48.6 | EU to Japan 28.9 | Japan to EU 53.9 |
| US to EU 98.1 | EU to US 97.4 | Japan to US 90.0 |

Exports in US$ billion (1993)

3 Study cartoon **E**
 a) What are
   i) tariffs, ii) quotas?
 b) How do tariffs and quotas work in favour of rich countries and against poor countries?
 c) What can poor countries do to try to increase their value of trade?

E

You have most of the world's trade, yet you impose tariffs and quotas to prevent us from selling our goods

We must protect our jobs and industries by limiting your cheap imports

Economically less developed countries 20% of world trade

Economically developed countries 80% of world trade

Summary Governments try to influence patterns of international trade by grouping together to establish trading blocs and by imposing tariffs, quotas and international commodities agreements.

▶ What are some of the recent trends in international trade? ◀

The Pacific Rim

The term 'Pacific Rim' has been applied to the earthquake and volcanic belt which surrounds the Pacific Ocean. Increasingly it is also being used to refer to that part of the world which has seen, since the 1980s, the most rapid economic growth. This growth has also extended to international trade (map B page 118).

Taken in its widest sense, the Pacific Rim includes all the countries which surround the Pacific Ocean and its adjacent seas (map **A**). Countries such as Singapore and South Korea are widely accepted as being part of the rim although neither face directly onto the Pacific. Likewise not all countries in the rim have experienced a rapid growth in GNP and trade. Although growth has, so far, been limited to a few countries, commentators seem to agree that the balance of trade is shifting from the Atlantic to the Pacific. Some of the recent trends in trade within the Pacific Rim are listed opposite.

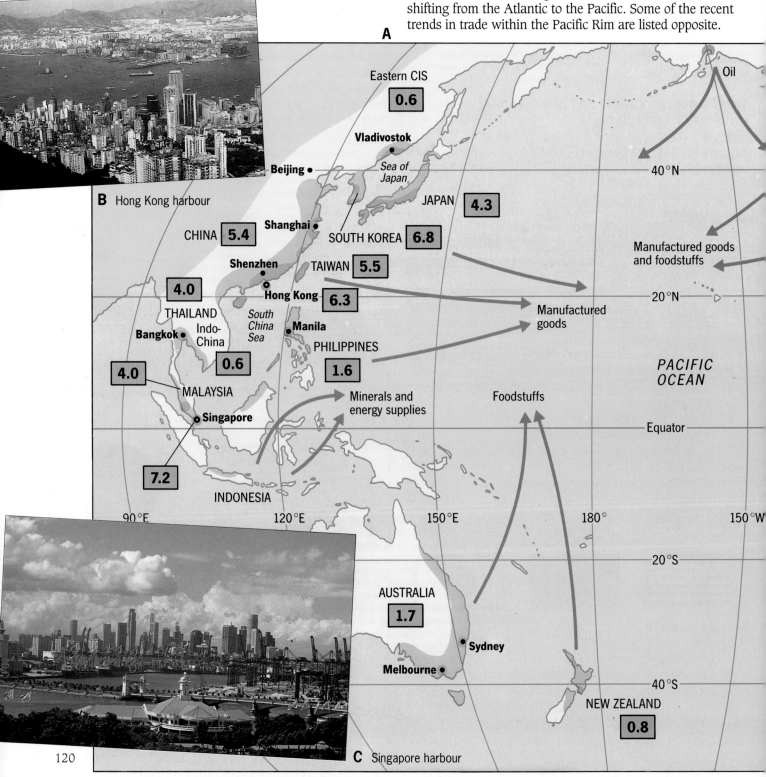

B Hong Kong harbour

C Singapore harbour

A

Eastern CIS 0.6

Vladivostok

Beijing ●   Sea of Japan   40°N

JAPAN 4.3

CHINA 5.4   Shanghai ●

SOUTH KOREA 6.8

Shenzhen   TAIWAN 5.5

4.0   ○ Hong Kong 6.3

Manufactured goods and foodstuffs

THAILAND   South China Sea   20°N

Bangkok ●   Indo-China   ● Manila

PHILIPPINES

0.6   1.6   Manufactured goods

4.0

MALAYSIA   Minerals and energy supplies

○ Singapore   Foodstuffs   PACIFIC OCEAN

Equator

7.2

INDONESIA

90°E   120°E   150°E   180°   150°W

20°S

AUSTRALIA

1.7

● Sydney

Melbourne ●

40°S

NEW ZEALAND

0.8

Oil

- Growth has been concentrated within a few countries and has not extended to much of Latin America or to parts of mainland Asia.
- Japan and the western USA experienced a rapid growth between 1950 and 1980 but since then the rate of growth has slowed.
- The countries with the fastest growing economies since 1980 are Hong Kong, Singapore (photo **C**), Taiwan and South Korea. They are threatening the former supremacy in the Pacific region of Japan and the USA.
- In other countries growth is limited to core areas e.g. Bangkok in Thailand, Manila in the Philippines and Shenzhen in South China.

- Most Asian countries lack the raw materials and energy resources needed for industry. Their trade therefore consists of importing these goods and exporting manufactured goods. This gives them a healthy trade balance surplus.
- The USA now shares more trade with Asia than it does with its traditional trading partners which now belong to the EU.
- Four of the world's busiest six ports are within the Pacific Rim.
- The economic recession of the early 1990s has reduced trade in this region as it has elsewhere in the world.

General Agreement on Trade and Tariffs (GATT)

The Uruguay round of the GATT negotiations began in 1986. The main hope was to create one large world free trade area which would replace the various protectionist blocs. Although some 150 nations were involved in the negotiations, most of the arguing and decision making was made by the G7 countries (Japan, Italy, France, Germany, UK, USA and Canada). The two major disputes were between

- the USA and the EU over farm subsidies;
- Japan and the remainder over tariffs since Japan discriminated against exports from other countries yet was free to export cars and electrical equipment to the rest of the world.

During most of the negotiations the developing countries, for which free trade is essential if they are to be allowed to sell their goods to developed countries, were often forced to watch events as spectators. It was perhaps only because all of the G7 leaders had to urgently improve their political image at home, that an agreement was finally reached in December 1993. The hope is that free trade will speed up the end of the world's economic recession, create more jobs and increase the volume of world trade. It is likely that, as usual, the developed countries will benefit the most.

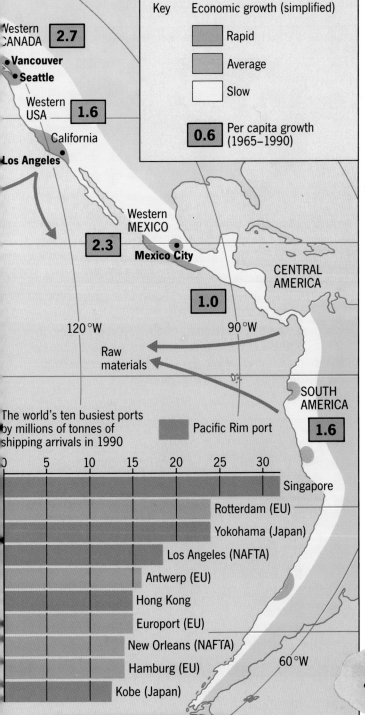

Activities

1 a) What is the Pacific Rim?
   b) Which two Pacific Rim countries used to have most wealth and trade?
   c) Which four Pacific Rim countries have developed their economies and trade the most since 1980?
   d) Name four large ports in the Pacific Rim. In which country is each port located?

2 a) i) What is the meaning of GATT?
      ii) What are the G7?
   b) Why were some countries
      i) in favour of the GATT proposals,
      ii) against the GATT proposals?

Summary Recent trends have seen a growth in trade between the Pacific Rim countries and a GATT agreement which should increase free trade and reduce protectionism.

121

Does your geography room have a globe? A globe shows the actual shape of the earth. You will notice that it is circular and has three dimensions. These two features, however, make it impossible to draw the earth accurately onto a flat piece of paper (see Activity 1). Parts of the map will either have the wrong **shape** or the wrong **size.**

Map projections result from the various attempts made to try to 'project' the three dimensional globe onto a two dimensional sheet of paper. Each map projection therefore has to be a compromise. The most suitable type of projection

depends upon what the **cartographer** (a person who draws maps) is trying to show.

Correct shape

In diagram **A**, which is a Mercator projection, the continents have been given their correct shape but their size (area) is wrong. This is because, while on a globe the poles appear as a point, on this projection they have been 'stretched' and so become as wide as the Equator. The further a place is from the Equator, the greater is the exaggeration of its size. The Mercator projection is still used by navigators as any straight line on the map has a constant bearing (direction).

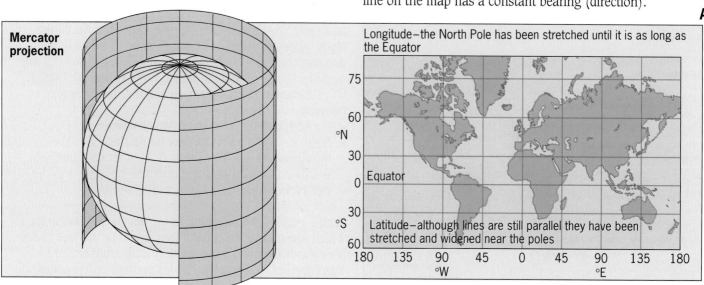

Mercator projection

A Longitude–the North Pole has been stretched until it is as long as the Equator

Equator

Latitude–although lines are still parallel they have been stretched and widened near the poles

Correct area (size)

In diagrams **B** and **C**, the Mollweide and Peters' projections, the continents have been given their correct size (area) but this time their shape is incorrect (distorted). The Peters' projection is becoming increasingly favoured for showing

developing countries in relation to developed countries. In order to get the size correct, the continents have had to be drawn narrower and longer. Equal area maps are used to show distributions, e.g. world population.

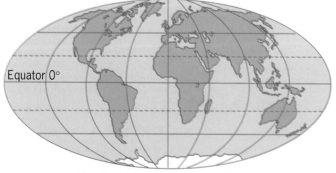

B Mollweide projection

Equator 0°

The lines of longitude are too curved

C Peters projection

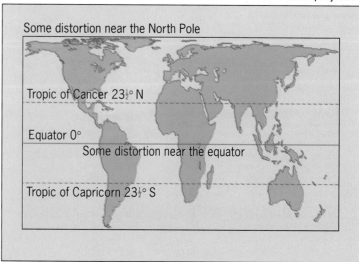

Some distortion near the North Pole

Tropic of Cancer 23½° N

Equator 0°

Some distortion near the equator

Tropic of Capricorn 23½° S

Correct distance

In diagram **D**, a zenithal projection, the scale is correct along any line drawn from the centre of the projection, but both the shapes and sizes of places are incorrect. (Zenith means a point directly overhead e.g. the position of the mid-day sun on the Equator, page 8). A map centred on the North Pole (or London as in diagram **E**) is effective for the northern hemisphere but greatly distorts places to the south of the Equator. This type of projection is useful for plotting air-routes as it shows the shortest distance, known as a great circle route, and the correct direction (bearing) between two places. One great circle route, between Europe and the Pacific countries, passes over the arctic. A map showing the Pacific Rim (pages 120 and 121) is a zenithal projection centred on the Pacific Ocean.

Compromise projections

Several projections used in an atlas try to compromise so that while neither the shape, the size nor the distance is correct, their distortion and exaggeration are minimised.

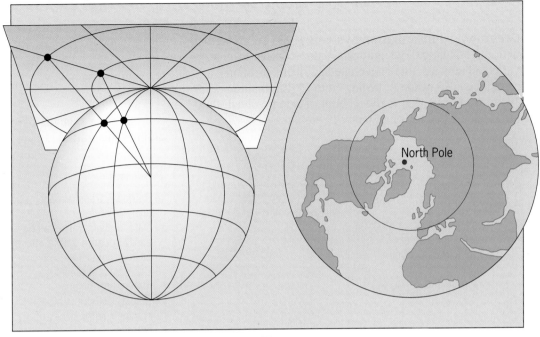

D Zenithal projection

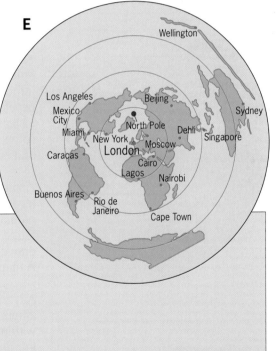

E

Wellington, Los Angeles, Beijing, Sydney, Mexico City, Miami, Dehli, Singapore, North Pole, New York, Moscow, Caracas, London, Cairo, Lagos, Nairobi, Buenos Aires, Rio de Janeiro, Cape Town

Activities

1 In an atlas the ball-shaped globe has to be projected on a flat surface. Is this possible?
   a) Peel an orange in one piece and try to lay the peel flat onto a piece of paper.
   b) Describe what happens to the peel, and say how many shapes you produced.

2 Match the types of projection shown opposite with the correct
   i) description and
   ii) use.

Peters'	shows the correct shape but size is greatly distorted	navigation
zenithal	shows the correct distances but size and shape are incorrect	air-routes
Mercator	shows the correct size but shape is greatly distorted	population distribution

3 Make a list of the various types of map projections used in your atlas. Try to divide them into those which have the correct shape, correct size, correct distances, or are a compromise between the three.

Summary

No atlas map can be totally accurate. All will have some good qualities such as correct shape, size or distance, but all will have limitations. The choice of a projection depends upon the purpose of a particular map.

► *What are Geographical Information Systems (1)?* ◄

Geographical Information Systems (GIS) are concerned with the handling of geographical data, collected from a variety of sources, and its storage in a digital form on computers. GIS need not be limited to IT (Information Technology) but, due to the amount of data involved, they are ideally suited to computers. GIS provides:

> A powerful set of tools for collecting, storing, retrieving at will, transforming and displaying spatial data from the real world for a particular set of purposes. (Burrough P.A.1986)

As with other systems GIS has inputs, process, stores and outputs (diagram **A**).

A

Inputs	Stores	Processes	Outputs
Data from a variety of sources. • Satellite images, aerial photos, Landsat images • Different types of map – OS maps, maps of soils, relief, settlement, etc • Digital data and graphs	a) Data stored in digital form b) Vast quantities of data	a) Retrieval, transformation and analysis of data b) Data in digital form can be easily updated (unlike atlases or textbooks) c) Can select and enlarge material for display d) Display colours can be changed at the press of a button	a) Several maps or sources of data can be displayed on the screen at the same time b) A final composite map is achieved by superimposing (overlays) several maps on each other c) Maps, graphs, tables

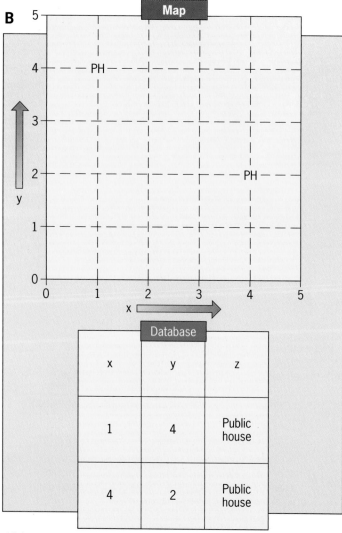

Principal role of GIS

The main role of GIS is to process raw geographical data in order to produce further information that can be used for informed decision making. This is achieved through the development of new and exciting ways of manipulating and displaying spatial data (maps), and by performing simple and complex spatial analysis on the geographical data quickly and efficiently.

A map is the traditional way of showing spatial data. A map records and displays geographical data by using (x,y) co-ordinates together with a (z) value that records the features found at each (x,y) location (diagram **B**). Maps are usually drawn on two-dimensional flat sheets of paper (page 122). A map, once drawn in an atlas, is difficult to update.

Advances in computer technology have enabled huge amounts of data to be stored in a **database**. A database within a GIS acts as a storage facility for geographical information. For example, diagram **B** shows a small database recording information for public houses. The computer can access this database, and display the spatial data using the (x,y) co-ordinates recorded and the associated (z) feature. On a standard two dimensional map, each (x,y) co-ordinate can only store and display, at the most, two (z) features (e.g. height of land and either soils, or settlement, or vegetation, etc). With improvements in technology, a computerised GIS can store hundreds of (z) features for each (x,y) location. These can then be selected depending upon the particular features the map is to display. It is also possible to display maps in three dimensions using a computer, with each (x,y) location recording a particular (z) height feature. Data can then be displayed using a range of graphics.

C

Map features

Data can be displayed on a map in one of three ways (diagram **D**).

Point	Line	Polygon
A point feature is displayed at one particular (x,y) location on the map.	A line consists of a series of (x,y) co-ordinatesthat join together, with each having the same (z) feature (e.g a railway line).	A polygon consists of a series of (x,y) co-ordinates that join together to complete a boundary. Everything inside this boundary is assigned the same (z) feature (e.g. a wood).

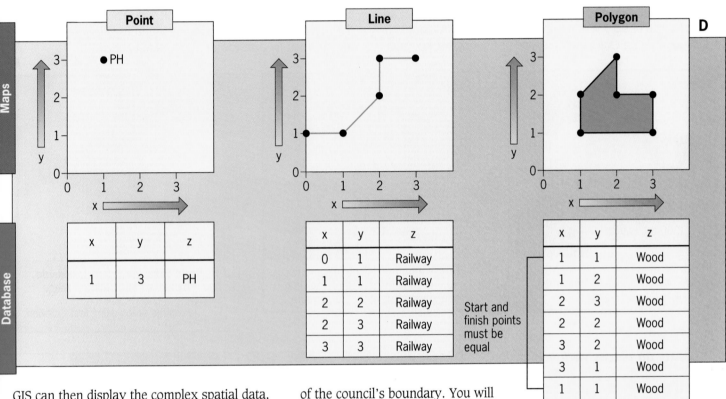

D

GIS can then display the complex spatial data, using the (x,y,z) values, and analyse it. Two of the most common techniques used for performing spatial analysis are **buffering** and **overlaying**. These techniques are described in the following section which seeks to select the ideal site for a rubbish dump.

Locating a rubbish dump

The local council have asked you to locate a suitable site for a new rubbish dump. The rubbish dump has to be located within the council boundary. In locating the new site, the council have specified the following requirements:

1 The site should be located at least 500 metres away from all urban areas.
2 The soil must be of poor quality.
3 The land should be sufficiently flat to allow easy vehicle access (slope of under 2°).

To identify the possible sites that satisfy the above criteria, you should first locate the extent of the council's boundary. You will then need the three maps which contain the relevant information. These maps, which should all be at same scale, will be a:

• settlement map highlighting the urban areas;
• soil map;
• slope angle map.

Each of the above criteria should then be examined in turn (pages 126-7).

examined in turn (pages 126-7).

Activities

1 a) What are Geographical Information Systems (GIS)?
  b) What are the main inputs, stores, processes and outputs of a GIS?
  c) What is the difference between a map and a data base?
  d) Why is a GIS of more value than an atlas?

Summary

A Geographical Information System (GIS) collects, stores, retrieves, analyses and displays geographical data. A wide range of maps, together with satellite images and aerial photographs, can be used to reveal spatial patterns and relationships.

►What are Geographical Information Systems (2)?◄

1 Locate all the places that lie at least 500 metres from an urban area   This involves a process called **buffering**. A boundary must be drawn around the limits of all the urban areas on the map. A minimum of 10 houses is needed to constitute an urban area. This produces a number of polygons (diagram **A**). Each polygon should then be studied in turn. From each point on the polygon boundary a second point has to be located 500 metres away, and at an exact angle of 90°. When this has been done you should be able to draw an exact replica shape of the original polygon

but at a distance of 500 metres from its boundary. The area between the urban area and the new polygon is referred to as the buffered zone.

Any point located **inside** the buffered zone, or inside the urban boundary, is considered unsuitable according to the council's criteria. Any point outside the buffered zones should be highlighted as a possible site. The map should then be traced onto a transparency and highlighting all those areas which lie **outside** of the buffered zones.

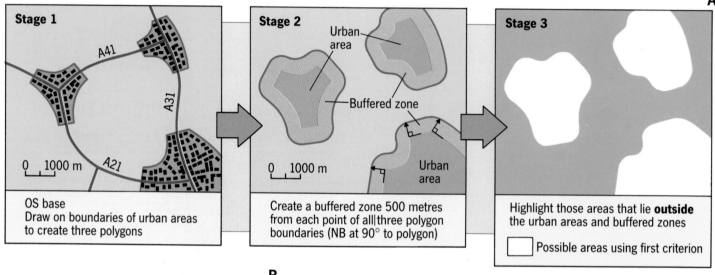

A

Stage 1

A41

A31

A21

0 1000 m

OS base
Draw on boundaries of urban areas
to create three polygons

Stage 2

Urban area

Buffered zone

Urban area

0 1000 m

Create a buffered zone 500 metres
from each point of all three polygon
boundaries (NB at 90° to polygon)

Stage 3

Highlight those areas that lie **outside**
the urban areas and buffered zones

☐ Possible areas using first criterion

2 Locate all places with poor soils
The soil map, needed to locate areas of poor soil, should have the same scale as the one previously used for highlighting the urban areas in Stage **1**. A line can be drawn on the map to show the boundary between good and poor quality soil (diagram **B**). This map should be traced onto a transparency in the same manner as in diagram **A**, with the poor soils highlighted.

3 Locate all areas of flat land   A slope angle map is needed to locate all those areas within the council's boundary that have, as specified by the council, a slope angle of under 2°. The map should be at the same scale as the previous maps. On it, a line can be drawn to indicate the boundary between land which has a slope greater and less than 2° (diagram **C**). The areas under 2°, indicating flat ground, can be highlighted and traced onto a third transparency.

B

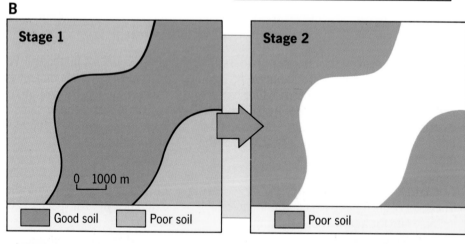

Stage 1

0 1000 m

☐ Good soil   ☐ Poor soil

Stage 2

☐ Poor soil

C

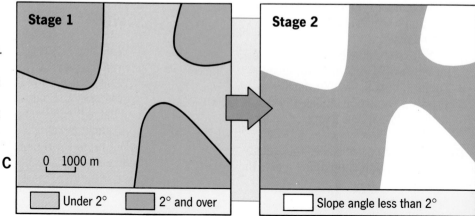

Stage 1

0 1000 m

☐ Under 2°   ☐ 2° and over

Stage 2

☐ Slope angle less than 2°

Overlaying the transparencies

To find the areas that satisfy the council's three specified criteria, the transparencies should be placed one on top of each other. This process, called **overlaying**, is a fundamental operation of a GIS (diagram **D**). It can only be performed, however, using maps that have the same scale and a common origin. The areas, in our example, that contain all three types of highlighting can then be isolated and traced onto a base map. This composite map can then be forwarded to the council as it fits their criteria and shows all the possible sites in which to locate the rubbish dump. It is possible to use many more overlays than just the three described in this example (e.g access roads, visibility of the dump from urban areas, direction of prevailing winds should the dump smell, soil permeability, etc).

Computer enhancement to highlight the best sites.

With improvements in computer technology, this process can be done much more efficiently and quickly than the manual method described, yet still using the same techniques. The computer performs the same operation by studying each criteria in turn. Those areas that satisfy one particular criteria are assigned the value 1, while those that fail to satisfy the criteria are given the value 0. Those areas of land within the council's boundary that obtain the value 3 are given the highest priority as they fit all three criteria, i.e. they are away from urban areas and are on poor soil and flat land. Areas that satisfy two of the three criteria are assigned the value 2 and are considered medium priority. Those areas with a value of 1 or 0 will be rejected.

GIS and the future

GIS has arisen from the joining of information technology and the demand for the storage and manipulation of data. Its strengths lie particularly in the ability to use it to 'model' geographical reality and to consider the impact of proposed or possible changes in spatial patterns in the natural or human environment. It is a technology where the role and value of geographers is beginning to be felt.

Source: Geographic Information Systems, *Geofile*, April 1993

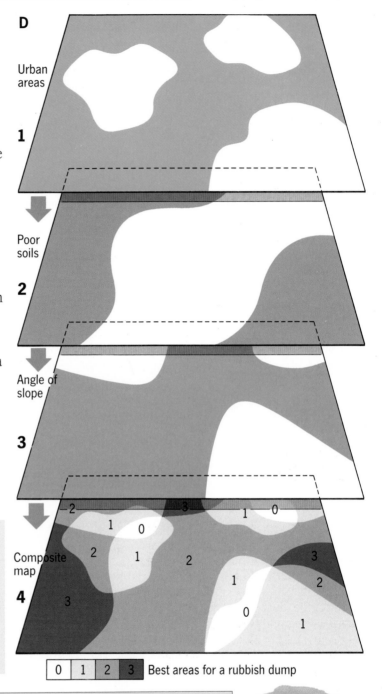

D

1 — Urban areas

2 — Poor soils

3 — Angle of slope

4 — Composite map

| 0 | 1 | 2 | 3 | Best areas for a rubbish dump

Activities

1 a) Attempt to locate a new rubbish dump within your own local council's boundary. (You may prefer, as an alternative to the rubbish dump, to try to locate the best possible site for some other feature such as a hypermarket, a caravan park or a windfarm.)
   You will need to find a range of maps some of which may use the same criteria as used on these two pages, some may use criteria that you can think of for yourselves.

   Complete the location exercise either manually or with the use of a computer.

   b) How effective do you think a geographical information system is when trying to produce a composite map to show the best possible sites for a new rubbish dump (or hypermarket, caravan park or windfarm)?

   c) What other uses can be made of geographical information systems?

Summary

Composite maps for specific purposes can be constructed by overlaying various distributions of thematic data that can be combined to show inter-relationships. This can be done either manually or with the help of a computer (information technology).

Index